Mission in Mufti

Recent Titles in
Contributions in Political Science

A Right to Bear Arms: State and Federal Bills of Rights and Constitutional Guarantees
Stephen P. Halbrook

The Politics of Economic Adjustment: Pluralism, Corporatism, and Privatization
Richard E. Foglesong and Joel D. Wolfe, editors

Policy through Impact Assessment: Institutionalized Analysis as a Policy Strategy
Robert V. Bartlett, editor

Behind the Uprising: Israelis, Jordanians, and Palestinians
Yossi Melman and Dan Raviv

From Feudalism to Capitalism: Marxian Theories of Class Struggle and Social Change
Claudio J. Katz

The Challenge of the Exception: An Introduction to the Political Ideas of Carl Schmitt between 1921 and 1936, Second Edition
George Schwab

The Demobilization of American Voters: A Comprehensive Theory of Voter Turnout
Michael J. Avey

Iran: From Royal Dictatorship to Theocracy
Mohammed Amjad

Managing Fiscal Strain in Major American Cities: Understanding Retrenchment in the Public Sector
William J. Pammer, Jr.

The Latin American Narcotics Trade and U.S. National Security
Donald J. Mabry, editor

Public Policy and Transit System Management
George M. Guess, editor

American Conservative Thought Since World War II: The Core Ideas
Melvin J. Thorne

Mission in Mufti

Brazil's Military Regimes, 1964–1985

Wilfred A. Bacchus

Contributions in Political Science, Number 255

GREENWOOD PRESS
New York • Westport, Connecticut • London

Library of Congress Cataloging-in-Publication Data

Bacchus, Wilfred A.
Mission in Mufti : Brazil's military regimes, 1964–1985 / Wilfred A. Bacchus.
p. cm.—(Contributions in political science, ISSN 0147–1066; no. 255)
Includes bibliographical references (p.)
ISBN 0–313–25535–0 (lib. bdg. : alk. paper)
1. Brazil—Politics and government—1964–1985. 2. Military government—Brazil—History—20th century. 3. Brazil—Armed Forces—Political activity—History—20th century. 4. Brazil—Economic conditions—1964–1985. I. Title. II. Series.
F2538.25B33 1990
322'.5'0981—dc20 89–26069

British Library Cataloguing in Publication Data is available.

Library of Congress Catalog Card Number: 89–26069
ISBN: 0–313–25535–0
ISSN: 0147–1066

First published in 1990

Greenwood Press, 88 Post Road West, Westport, Connecticut 06881
An imprint of Greenwood Publishing Group, Inc.

Printed in the United States of America

The paper used in this book complies with the Permanent Paper Standard issued by the National Information Standards Organization (Z39.48–1984).

10 9 8 7 6 5 4 3 2 1

Copyright Acknowledgments

The author and publisher thank the following for permission to use material from: "Development under Military Rule," by Wilfred Bacchus, in *Armed Forces & Society*, Claude E. Welch, Jr., ed., 12 (1986); "Long-term Military Rulership in Brazil," by Wilfred Bacchus, in *Journal of Political & Military Sociology* 13 (1985); and "Controlled Political Transition in Brazil," by Wilfred Bacchus, in *Liberalization and Redemocratization in Latin America*, George A. Lopez and Michael Stohl, eds. (Greenwood Press, Westport, CT 1987), Copyright © 1987 by George A. Lopez and Michael Stohl.

Contents

Figures and Tables

FIGURE

TABLES

Acknowledgments

My greatest indebtednesses, both in numbers and in depth, are to the many Brazilians—only a few identified by name in the text, due to the long-term sensitivity of their viewpoints—who so very generously gave of their time and wisdom to me, always in the interest of an honest interpretation of the Brazilian reality of the past decades. Many North American academics' first encounter with the warmth and intelligent vitality of the Brazilian personality has come through personal introductions or vacation travels. My introduction to Brazil resulted from a wise counselor who led me to choose Portuguese for study at the U.S. Naval Academy, and it then flowered under Professors Walsh and Hefler.

My research efforts in Brazil have been aided by Professors Helio Jaguaribe and Candido Mendes, and the latter's staff of the Faculty (now University) Candido Mendes. Professors Alexandre Barros of IUPERJ and Geraldo Halfeld of the ESG were very helpful in my study of the Escola Superior de Guerra. Library staff members at the Getulio Vargas Foundation and Army Headquarters in Rio de Janeiro, and at the Interamerican Defense College in Washington repeatedly assisted me in the literature analyses by which I examined elite ideology. Along the way, tangible assistance for the project has come from the Research Council of the University of Connecticut and from Muhlenberg College.

Special thanks go to Professor Fred Turner of the University of Connecticut for encouraging me and then guiding me initially as I began this study. I benefitted much from the anonymous comments of reviewers for the journals cited in chapters 3 and 4 leading to publications of earlier versions of the elite ideology studies, and to the study of redemocratization which has appeared as a contributed chapter in an earlier Greenwood book. By the extensive bibliographic note credits, it will be obvious to all how much I have depended upon the seminal works of Professors Skidmore and Stepan for background and orientation in this study. Even so, and to an unusual extent I believe, this study has been a rather isolated endeavor. It was motivated by the perception that most of my fellow countrymen, even those in academe, have not fully appreciated nor fairly assessed the earnest "mission" undertaken in 1964 by Brazil's military leadership. Those few men and their successors over the twenty-one years never saw their role as mere caretakers of their country's massive enterprise, and certainly not as its exploiters. I hope this rendering of what faced them by way of problems, possibilities, and accomplishments has balanced criticism of some misspent opportunities with tokens of my great admiration of their perseverance, integrity, and dedication to their nation.

A final acknowledgment is of deep appreciation to my wife, who knows better than anyone else how much I have depended upon not only her constant support but wise counsel and suggestions throughout the two decades of this project's slow evolution. As expected, I contend that any errors of fact or insight that remain in this work are no one's responsibility but mine.

Introduction

The powerful bias against military authoritarian governments seems one of the first points this study should recognize as something which is prevalent in the western industrialized world. In the broadest sense, I share such attitudes, which are perhaps nowhere more firmly established than in academic circles. Thus, it is not the intent of this study of Brazil's lengthy authoritarian period in the latter half of the present century to undertake to reverse that prejudice. However, out of my years of scrutiny, I find the Brazilian example quite unique, and unrepresentative of the many contemporary military regimes which were so numerous in Latin America during the 1970s. This study focuses on unique features of that ruling system, its policies and administrative mechanisms, issues and obstacles it faced, and in summation the evaluation of the degree of success it obtained in the "mission" undertaken.

In recognition of economic advances made in the last decades, Brazil has been designated as a "newly industrialized country," but in terms of political maturity, one ought to regard it as being still in transition toward democracy, if not even in suspended status. Transfer of ruling power to an indirectly elected, civilian-led government from an opposition political party can be seen as a significant step; yet there is reason to doubt the extent to which the military leadership has withdrawn to the barracks. Naturally, they resisted (unsuccessfully) the abolition of the former clause in the 1946 constitution granting them guarantor status of ruling authority during times of political crisis. Even so, military ministers enjoy favored prominence in the Sarney administration.

When the Sarney administration entered office, it was under extraordinarily difficult circumstances, politically, economically, and even spiritually. Brazilians, so notably buoyant even during times of trial or austerity, expected a well-known and much-loved, experienced civilian leader—Tancredo Neves, septuagenarian Minas Gerais governor and a former premier—to take over, and to solve the heavy problems of external indebtedness and imminent recession. Instead, he was lying on the operating table the evening before inauguration day, no longer able to endure the pain of his bleeding ulcers. When he died a few weeks later, after increasingly serious and desperate operations to save his life, Brazil had as president a relatively unknown man who had been placed on the opposition ticket in order to give balance and appeasement to conservatives, including the hard-line faction of the military elite. Sarney had until mid–1984 been a Democratic Socialist Party (PDS) senator and party leader who had defected only when he could no longer stave off nomination of the highly controversial and reputedly corrupt ex-Paulista Governor Paulo Maluf. This book is not about the Sarney government, however; it deals only with how the military elite dealt with the matter of transferring ruling power to a presidential team not of their choice.

By design, this study of the 1964–1985 period covers each of five successive but distinctively different presidencies, all of which came from the uppermost echelon of the army as active, four-star generals. It attempts to provide a detailed and accurate relation of events under each regime that can be used by history students. Graduate and undergraduate political science students will most logically use it as a detailed case study of military regimes of the Third World, encompassing problems of civil-military relations, bureaucratic behavior within military elites and in tandem with technocrats, and developmental planning and administration in authoritarian systems. It covers the changing pattern of relations between countries such as Brazil—capable of trade and economic rivalry with the developed world nations—and their long-lived, strong friendship with the United States. To meet both design objectives presents the challenge of combining topical analyses with historical context and occasionally a bit of background. Doing so without too many retrogressions in a rather small monograph adds to the problem.

Authoritarian political regimes headed by military leaders are so commonplace in the Third World that uninvited comparisons to other countries and their military regimes are inevitable. Eric Nordlinger (1977: 6) has observed that military authoritarianism is one of the most characteristic aspects of non-Western politics, accounting for well over half of the governing systems of Asia, Africa and Latin America in recent years. Within that broad range of regime types, one ordinarily asks where Brazil's 1964–1985 governments belong. Roy Macridis, (1986: 227–35) identifying three major prototypes—direct rule, indirect rule, and the shadowy cryptomilitary democracies—covered all bets by placing Brazil at various times within each but not, however, clarifying times and durations of passage within those three types.

Most observers agree that some form of direct rule applied in Brazil during much of Costa e Silva's brief tenure, and portions of the Médici and Geisel governments, when decree powers without the approval of the Congress were assumed. However, one could only equate the Brazilian governments over those twenty-one years to contemporary dictatorships in the developing Third World by overlooking the significant role numerous civilians, occupying cabinet-level positions of power, played in each Brazilian regime. The Congress and highest courts likewise had sufficient authority to overrule or challenge military decisions, except those concerning the succession process. It is true that the military elite exercised veto power on the important national issues, and on measures judged to involve their vital interests or to threaten "national security," broadly defined. However the military has enjoyed a similar span of privileges for many years in civilian-led governments. Indeed, Brazil has been ruled by a civil-military duopoly since 1946, if not for most of the century since it became a republic.

One could easily conclude, from perusing news items published by the North American press, that Brazilians suffered continuously from 1964 through 1985 under a typical military dictatorship. It is true that the lower class and a smaller middle class have been deprived not only of income growth comparable to national economic growth but of political participation as well. These were not democracies, of course, but were they dictatorships? Important differences with other military regimes chosen for comparison will emerge, upon examining evidence of the need which each regime had for nonmilitary bases of support, when each leader faced factional opposition from hard-liners, or from moderates, as one administration followed its contrary-minded rival.

Recent interpretations of the trend of military interventions in governments, particularly South American, such as the Guillermo O'Donnell (1973) "bureaucratic authoritarian" construct, have often placed the Brazilian military regimes at the head of a list of assumed imitators, disguising significant differences of style and actual behavior among those which followed. The military governing systems, all of shorter duration and uncertain stability, created in the 1966–1976 period in Argentina, Bolivia, Chile, Peru, Ecuador and Uruguay typified the former, "strong man" era of *caudillos* much more than they resembled Brazil's five military regimes. For example, the presidents' terms in office were terminated, and successors tapped, not by means of a consensus of military chiefs and at the preestablished times, but by challengers' interventions amidst faltering political and economic circumstances. Chile's lengthy Pinochet government is, of course, the significant exception, but it too bears little resemblance to the Brazilian governments. As O'Donnell and Philippe Schmitter (1986: IV–45) expressed this difference, absence of a military and political "pact" in each of those countries adversely affected transition of ruling power, in contrast to Brazil's record. They attributed Brazil's comparative success in the economic realm to "the firm and inordinately enduring control that its transitional governments have been able to keep on the process."

The most natural tendency is to associate economic successes produced in Brazil's second and third military governments with a comparatively rigid authoritarianism which existed from 1967 through 1973, and the accompanying infusion of foreign—especially American—investment capital. Undoubtedly that linkage has validity, but those two factors needed to be coupled with application of a well-drawn governmental design—that is, a coherent strategy for accelerated industrialization and national economic development—and a broad administrative renewal begun in the first regime under Gen. Humberto Castello Branco. One of the major features of that renewal was the transfer of the federal government from Rio de Janeiro to Brasilia. Whereas the Kubitschek and Goulart governments had attempted to initiate multiple-year planning and the separation of the Congress and federal bureaucracy from the Copacabana-Ipanema playground, each had made little real progress when they left office.

I am not, in fact, charmed by the rigidities and artificialities of Latin Americans' growing resort to centralized planning processes. Yet one can hardly deny that a large part of the Brazilian success—until the advent of the 1980s hyperinflation spurred by petroleum-based import costs and the staggering external debt burden—owed much to the effectiveness of governmental planning and execution introduced by the Castello Branco regime and continued in the Costa e Silva and Médici governments. Comparable effectiveness and greater political stability in the fourth (Geisel) and fifth (Figueiredo) governments may have produced even greater economic success, had it not been for Brazil's boom-ending trade imbalance and stagflation. This came about as a direct consequence of the OPEC nations' drastic increase in oil prices, which severely affected Brazil because imports more than four-fifths of its crude oil. One need not look far beyond that one factor to appreciate the way it unhitched the regime's investment and expansion plans.

It would be unrealistic to expect, in this brief, focused study, to clarify all of the many questions raised about the regimes which governed Brazil over the twenty-one-year span that ended in 1985. I have chosen to concentrate upon examining the organization and the record established in that period, with some attention to the ideologic tendencies and internal divisions within the military elite. I chose the term "mission" for the title of the book because I believe that the leaders felt they were departing upon an uncharacteristic, duty-oriented commitment to the people of Brazil—a nonmilitary mission—when they seized the reins of the government from President Goulart in 1964. The other part of the title, mufti, also relates to what appeared unique: each incumbent in the presidency severed his hierarchical control over armed forces permanently by retirement from active duty, donning civilian clothes and never thereafter appearing again in his uniform.

I have consciously avoided the territory so capably examined in two recent works by well-known American Brazilianists, Thomas E. Skidmore and Alfred Stepan. The relating of major events of the twenty-one-year military-ruler era is sequential only within chapters and only briefly outlines events, factors behind decisions, and problems that were not intended for analysis. Skidmore's *The Politics of Military Rule in Brazil, 1964–85* offers a more comprehensive and detailed account from a different point of view, and it has not dealt with some areas that are covered in this book. If one seeks motives behind the military elite's deliberate decision to return ruling power to civilian hands, Alfred Stepan's seminal monograph comparing Brazil to other authoritarian systems of the Southern Cone, *Rethinking Military Politics*, takes up this question well beyond where this book stops, at the end of the Figueiredo government.

Within the parameters of this study, the central focus is on what the military elite sought to accomplish by taking control for the first time, and an assessment of what was achieved. It also considers what obstacles the regimes could not overcome, and where that resistance came from in each of the five regimes. These major questions raise many others, such as, What motivated those military leaders and their closest supporters? Was discipline in the military elite affected adversely? Did that sense of discipline and solidarity instead serve as a bonus to the regime's effective pursuit of its aims? Was sociopolitical ideology important? Was the widespread orientation toward anticommunism significant and of importance throughout the two decades? In contrast to the more nationalist ("third option") tendencies of the Vargas, Kubitschek, and Goulart governments, was the pro-Americanism of the first regime under Castello Branco characteristic of those which followed? Did the Escola Superior de Guerra (ESG), originated and for a time modeled after the U.S. National War College, sustain a pro-American bias?

Regarding the accomplishments of the five regimes, several further questions are taken up in subsequent chapters. How did the national economy fare under authoritarian, military direction? As greater earned wealth became available, how was it employed? On what basis was the decision taken to suspend governmental effort to redistribute wealth and income opportunity to the lower class workers and the unemployed? Were better economic and foreign investment opportunities created, and for whom? How did Brazil become the most indebted Third World state?

Did the lengthy authoritarian era expire by consensus of the wishes of the military elite, or was it under heavy attack? Finally, what relevant observations can be drawn from this study, and how might they be applicable to other rapidly developing states? If the Brazilian case is unique, as suggested here, what lessons can be gained to guide future regimes led by military elites under similar circumstances?

In the chapters that follow, I have chosen to move more or less chronologically after the first chapter, which attempts to identify the factors which unified and motivated the Brazilian armed forces to remove President Goulart and to retain authority under an unelected president from their own ranks. The following chapters explore some sequential themes, such as the role of the ESG—so often credited with primary importance—as the mentor and initiator of national policy-making under the military regimes; the degree and direction of service-and seniority-based ideologic divisions in each regime; and the deeper ideologic splits between pro-American moderates and independence-minded authoritarians regarding the nation's needs—for example, industrialization/urbanization, and eradication of radical, anti-regime insurgencies. Subsequent chapters take up the five regimes' policies and progress on national development and industrialization. The process of transition toward democratization, promised by each military president upon entering office, is pursued as a penultimate study of the delicate problem of political disengagement. Last, there is a summarization and post-era assessment, presumably aided by the perspective afforded after several years' passage of time.

Mission in Mufti

1

Unifying Factors Within the 1964 Military Movement

Without going into great detail concerning the Vargas legacy and the increasing politicization of the Brazilian military elite since the end of World War II, which was well explained in the work of Thomas Skidmore (1967) and Alfred Stepan (1971), a few brief points of background warrant mention here. First, let it be noted that political activity tends to peak and polarize (including within the military hierarchy) in the year or so preceding election of a new president and Congress. Brazil was to hold such an election in the late months of 1965, and rumors were swirling around the possibility—unconstitutional, even though President Goulart had not been elected head of state but vice president—that "Jango" was aiming for reelection. Second, as we stated in the introductory chapter, the Brazilian military elite had come to expect consultation and, perhaps, even veto powers over such highly important questions as the acceptability of a presidential candidate. Third, civilian politicians fully anticipated that any intervention on the part of the army would be brief, as had been the case in 1945, 1954, and 1961. And, finally, there was indeed disunity within the senior military elite and their followers, over communism/anticommunism, attitudes toward nationalism (and toward the United States to a degree), and over how and whether political actions and interventions might be justified.

Observers have tended to agree that two military factions supported Goulart's continuation in office till his successor had been elected. Taking his side for personal gain and, perhaps, ideological solidarity as well, was the "leftist-nationalist group" headed by those whom Goulart had chosen for top-level posts and for promotions, who stood by him until the end. There was a significantly larger group, ideologically neutral or tending toward a nationalist stance, who have been variously labeled "legalists" or the "barracks group," essentially disinclined to intervene in political matters, and concerned about public opposition to the military which had followed prior military interventions.

With such resistance even to intervention, to say nothing of taking political control over a lengthy period, it is only natural to ask why and how the "revolutionary movement" of 1964 came to be the answer to resolving the disorder which the Goulart government had created. Why did attitudes shift, especially among the "barracks group"? After a thorough, well-documented analysis, Alfred Stepan (1978a: 111, 132–33) concluded that the major factor was "a micro-political failure" in the quality of leadership and style of President Goulart and his inner circle of advisers. That conclusion, closely related to Huntington's political decay thesis, does not exclude the probability that other factors were relevant.

Other observers such as Miguel Arrães (1972), Teotônio dos Santos (1974), Abelardo Jurema (1964), and Fernando Pedreira (1964) saw the military elite's motive as mainly personal ego and collective gain for the services. Their assumptions, although they appeared plausible, are refuted by Stepan's (1988: 57, 72–81) data and interviews, which showed that Brazil's military expenditures and resources, unlike those of other authoritarian regimes, did not grow in real terms but actually declined under military rule. It was also made clear that they had desired more than they had received.

The other leading explanation offered to explain the unity behind the 1964 military power play is discussed in essays by Jan K. Black (1977), Rene Dreifuss (1981), Phyllis Parker (1977), and Edmar Morel (1965), each of whom found the answer in the close relationship between leading Brazilian conspirators (military and civilian) and corresponding elites in the United States. Essentially, Brazil was depicted as being the proxy of U.S. political and business interests who were overly concerned about Brazil's leftist course, feared that a sub rosa communist conspiracy was afoot, and willingly snuffed out democracy to protect their own selfish interests. Coming only four years after Cuba had fallen into the Soviet orbit, authors such as those had no problem in presenting a convincing thesis for the "Brazilian revolution," amounting in their view to a counter-revolution.

There is of course validity in each of these explanations, but yet there is some exaggeration of the essence of their motivations, which were not subject to one simplistic interpretation but, in fact, complementary to each other. Where various observers saw red (or at least pink), olive green, or red, white, and blue, I believe there was a veritable rainbow of attitudes responsible for the intervention. A case could be made that perception of an economic collapse was the primary factor, especially when accompanied by visions of apocalyptic social conflict from an increasingly aroused and organized lower class. Despite his immense land holdings, Goulart never enjoyed support from the conservative parties; consequently, as his influence declined, it became necessary for him to turn to the landless peasants and laborers for a political base. These he courted near the end by issuing increasingly radical decrees.

THE REMOVAL OF PRESIDENT GOULART

There is some sense of approaching tragedy in the events, widely reported in numerous works, leading to the deposition of João Goulart. His lone victory, overwhelming approval of a return to a presidential form of government, came despite backing of his party leadership and the Congress as a result of measures the president and his ministers took to demonstrate the political impasse and dire consequences that would result from a military-dictated parliamentary system that curtailed his authority. After approval by a five-to-one margin in a January 1963 referendum, one might have assumed that Goulart held a strong popular mandate. In fact, he was unable to move through the Congress his measures designed to broaden the political base through populistic appeals. Moreover, his opponents within the administrative-level bureaucracy did not allow circumvention of the legal impediments.

After the abortive "Sergeants' Revolt" in Brasilia, which took place in September 1963, and the crumbling of the Furtado economic plan for the remainder of Goulart's term in office, the president was no longer popular with either the left or right wings of the political spectrum. Dreifuss (1981: 102, 165, 205–6) and other observers have attempted to show that a U.S.-backed conspiracy was at work behind the scene, worried over Goulart's growing radicalism and planning what was increasingly seen as an urgently necessary action to rescue Brazil from chaos and, perhaps, also from Castroite communism.

With only weak political support for his government within the Congress, the bureaucracy, and the military hierarchy, Goulart set out to build alternative bases within two relatively powerless constituencies: labor and the student organization. The latter, under his minister of education's sponsorship, elected a newly radicalized leadership to the National Students Union (UNE) which, in the face of government inaction on university reform proposals as well as official prohibition of national-level meetings, turned to violent demonstrations. Students also infiltrated the ranks of the career-oriented organizations of noncommissioned officers (NCOs) of the army, navy (including the marine corps), and air force, to attempt to unionize and radicalize them. Those activities intensified after failure of the Brasilia "Sergeants' Revolt" of 1963, and provided some of the leadership for the naval mutiny in Rio de Janeiro of March 1964—the last dramatic event which put final nails in the coffin of the president. Quartim (1971: 174) identified the ringleaders of those revolutionary attempts as communists, one or two of whom became guerrilla chiefs operating in central Brazil several years later.

Students in Brazil, as in France and other countries, also sought to link themselves with the labor movement's tepidly radical factions. Peter Flynn (1979: 236, 252), among many others, found the radicals of the Brazilian labor movement to be similarly tied to the Brazilian Communist Party (PCB), which although outlawed was nevertheless politically active. Among Goulart's controversial acts, the sanctioning of a General Labor Congress (CGT) produced the greatest concern among his opponents. Whereas there was unusually firm governmental regulation and control over labor unions on an industry-wide, regional or state-level basis, so that arbitration and approval of strike action was always required, the CGT could now unify union workers nationally, potentially presenting the president with an effective counterweight to military demands. The further unionization of the NCOs would complete the political neutralization of political opposition to presidential initiatives on the part of the senior military leadership. Whether such a plan would have been effective cannot be known, because Goulart had already too nakedly challenged the armed forces to achieve his ultimate objectives. It is reasonable to judge that the connection between the UNE, the CGT, and the communists was well known within the right-wing opposition. Furthermore, in the newborn confidence of high-level sponsorship, and with the further aggravation of accelerated monetary deflation, the country was beset by waves of unauthorized strikes—even rumors of an imminent general strike to bring down Congress—to add to the fear of a Bolshevized revolution or a Castro-backed guerrilla campaign. Those fears were focused upon the emerging threat of communism in the northeast region, where radicals and eventually the Catholic Church and state governments competed to establish peasant organizations, following Francisco Julião's sudden success in organizing the Peasant Leagues. We shall turn to a detailed examination of that phenomenon in the following pages.

In the near absence of orderly, prosaic, and reliable managerial knowledge available to handle the new radicals, there was only one government institution (and no known academic counterpart) with a store of information and plans for solving socioeconomic and policy questions: the Escola Superior de Guerra. As we shall find in the following chapter, it had valuable studies on the Northeast.

THE SECURITY THREAT IN THE NORTHEAST

Perceptions of a dangerous threat to the political order were accentuated in November 1961, by the assembling of 1,600 delegates from all over the nation at the first National Peasants Congress at Belo Horizonte, sponsored by the president. With 40 percent of the agricultural population landless, and with the presence of communist agitators in the Northeast, it was inevitable that the Cold Warriors of Brazil and the United States should view such events with increasing anxiety. Since peasant activism was encouraged by Goulart, opponents were forced to work through external channels to formulate measures to contain the threat.

The leadership of this peasant congress fell naturally to a once-obscure lawyer from Pernambuco named Francisco Julião, who rose to prominence as the originator of the Northeast's Peasant Leagues. Julião's real name, Francisco Juliano Paula de Arruda, had been abbreviated, in the fashion of a "nom de guerre," before he acquired his national reputation. That reputation came about after startling success in a local court, defending the right of peasants at a plantation named Gallileia, located near his own property, in their bid to organize to defend collective rights.

Given the unmilitant attitudes previously displayed toward authority by peasants in Brazil and in most other countries, it would be natural to count organization of peasant unions as inconsequential. Knowledgeable Brazilians such as Gilberto Freyre (1967) and academics with specific insights about peasant culture in the Northeast such as Allen Johnson (1971) agree that the *Nordestino* peasants were passive and usually loyal to their masters. There were, of course, ample reasons for peasants of northeastern Brazil to be discontent with their lot. Yet, for sources such as Manuel de Andrade (1980), Shepard Forman (1975), Cynthia Hewitt (1969), Joseph Page (1972), Moacir Palmeira (1979), Kit Taylor (1978), or Mary Willkie (1964), there was hesitance to entrust representation of their cause to any unfamiliar persons, or even to new types of organizations. On the other hand, there were two well-known Northeasterners, Miguel Arrães (1972) and Josué de Castro (1969), who believed the peasants were ready to be led even into armed confrontation with the authorities, if that became necessary in the struggle to obtain economic justice.

The question of whether peasant organizations posed a real threat to the government is obviously important to the following discussion of how the military elite judged their position and the intentions of the Goulart government. I have real doubts that the Peasant Leagues actually posed a danger to the preservation of governing authority, based upon my own observations some years later, including my exposure to Francisco Julião in a series of seminars given at Ivan Illich's CIDOC Center in Cuernavaca during the summer of 1969. To me, he appeared uncharismatic and a most unlikely revolutionary figure, but I must acknowledge that he had been imprisoned preceding his flight from Brazil and may have changed greatly during that time. The other point to note is that he was widely seen as a security threat, not only by civil and military authorities in the region but even abroad.

Consciousness-raising and Peasant Organizing Work

Before describing how the Peasant Leagues and rival church and state organizations grew so rapidly in the early 1960s, it should be appreciated that voting rights, as handled by landlords and plantation managers in the Northeast, presented a special kind of empowerment of the upper class and the conservative politicians. As successive laws under the Vargas *Estado Novo* dictatorship and postwar legislatures broadened the franchise, those who then held power had to adopt new measures to maintain control. With peasants totally dependent upon their bosses, it was easy to develop what became a "herded voting" system which only reinforced the stronghold of the dominant landlords (Flynn 1979: 34, 258). On election day, foremen brought truckloads of semiliterate hands and sharecroppers to the polling place, usually preceded by a festive day of free drinks. Then each voter dutifully dropped a printed ballot, supervised by the foreman, into the urn, guaranteeing that there would be no political change for another several years. The real irony of that system, for the genuine reformers who drafted laws to extend the voting rights, was that it actually reinforced old rigidities by increasing representation in the Northeast—always the country's conservative base in Congress—by extending the vote to formerly disenfranchised, propertyless peasants everywhere. In the Northeast, the growth of voter rolls was dramatic.

Efforts to arouse the peasants from their passive stoicism had begun through Catholic priests and lay workers in the region, many years before the Peasant League phenomenon began. Emanuel de Kadt (1970) has provided a good picture of the activities of those "consciousness-raisers" in the study of the Basic Education Movement (MEB). Literacy education efforts took a further swing upward with the introduction of Paulo Freire's "method"—worked out in the extension education division of the Rural Pernambuco University, a state-funded institution. The activities of the "Paulo Freire Method" alphabetizers are described below. While both were effective, it is the church, through its mainly non-Brazilian clergy, which has proven more enduringly dedicated to peasant activism, still being pursued in both rural and urban settings through its many thousand "base communities" organizations.

In an unintended way, U.S. sugar policy, developed in the wake of Fidel Castro's 1961 expropriations offensive, had a significant role in lending impetus to the rural unionization movement in Brazil. Before 1961, the sugar-growing estates of the Northeast had been declining in value and productivity and in the capability to compete for world markets. The reallocated U.S. quotas led many landlords to a renewed interest in their plantations. Some had converted to cattle raising, and many of the least progressive no longer maintained much control over how their plantations were being used. On many occasions, scores of landless squatters had semilegal claims of resident rights on land worked for many years with a landlord's approval, or at least by absence of any objection. Now, with profitability in prospect, processes of eviction and even murder of resisting tenants began to occur, carried out by hired gunmen employed by the patron as a private militia. Indeed, it was as a lawyer advocate for the *moradores* of the Gallileia estate in Pernambuco that Francisco Julião got his first fame as a peasant union organizer.

Popularization of the Peasant Leagues (*Ligas Campesinas*) came about not from Julião's initiative, but through civic leaders and the conservative regional news media, intending to alert others to a new danger. The same title had been used in 1945, during the brief interval when the Brazilian Communist Party (PCB) enjoyed legal status, to designate organizations of landless laborers that they planned to establish. When Julião's Leagues were reborn in the mid–1950s, and until the official sponsorship of the Goulart regime began in 1961, very little notice and importance was attached to these semiradical organizations. It was only after Julião, with Goulart's blessing, led in the convening of the Peasants Congress at Belo Horizonte—capital of the important Minas Gerais state—that efforts to organize peasants and sharecroppers really took off. Soon thereafter, with Castroism a daily concern in the United States, Julião's name became well known in Brazil and abroad, with a series of feature articles and a televised special report published in 1963 publicizing his rise.

Julião at various times, before sympathetic followings, declared himself to be a Marxist; and he never voiced objection when he was so named by others. As others (Forman 1975: 186–88, 270–71; Page 1972: 39–50, 78–92) have pointed out in the context of Northeast Brazilian politics, honorable representatives of the working class were exceptional if they did not call themselves Marxists, but in so doing, they were not normally also associating themselves with membership in a communist organization per se. The connection to Castro-type communism was far stronger in Julião's case; he became a devoted follower and frequent visitor of Fidel Castro. After the 1964 military coup, and Julião's exile to Cuernavaca, other observers (Flynn 1979; Forman 1975) felt that he had become more radical in his views, but—as already noted—I judged him to be relatively unmilitant.

Activities and Problems of the Peasant League Movement

Organizational efforts, including the recruiting of new groups of landless workers, intensified after the late 1961 Peasants Congress at Belo

Horizonte, and had not crested by the time of the military takeover in 1964. Julião's Leagues had a lengthy head start and local recognition, but he soon began to feel increasing competition from the church and state organizations. To continue recruiting, Julião's League organizers found it necessary to resort to such "threatening" moves as demonstrations, rallies, and marches on town halls. Counteraction came first from landowners' militia, but in time also from the police, state troops, and the Fourth Army's local contingents. Some were peacefully dispersed, but a few of the more radical League marches led to bloody confrontations.

With the increasing violence, including Army efforts—apparently contrary to what Goulart's generals in Rio de Janeiro were instructing—to discourage Julião's recruiting activities, there was evident need for strong guidance from the top. Instead, by the last few months of 1962, Julião was mostly absent from the scene, campaigning for a federal deputy's seat representing an interior district of Pernambuco state. The absence became permanent in January, 1963, when he moved to Rio de Janeiro as an elected deputy, with every indication that his ambitions stretched far beyond the Northeast, even to national and international horizons. As a consequence, internal decay and misdirection grew within the top level of the Peasant League organization. The so-called "Dianapolis Caper" of mid–1962 to December of that year is a useful illustration of the harm done to his movement by his inattention to leadership duties, even though it should be noted that this incident did not take place within the nine northeast region states, but in Goiana, in the center of the nation.

The Dianapolis project was the first of a number of guerrilla centers—the common term was *foco*—in the northeast and central regions of Brazil which were expected to begin a major guerrilla offensive starting on or about May 1, 1963. The plan fell apart after a coordinated Fourth Army and state police raid on the foco at Dianapolis in December 1962. The coordinator of the Dianapolis project was Clodomiro Morães, one of Julião's chief League subordinates who had begun as a Peasant League recruiter but then shifted to university students, particularly those at the University of Brasilia, which was relatively close to the chosen site at Dianapolis, Goiana. It was seen as strategically located, yet in a comparatively less inhabited area. The actual location was an abandoned property and hamlet near Dianapolis; when taken over, the "farm" was given the cover name of "Capitalist Company of the Northeast," which was to be further applied to additional centers in the interior of such northeastern states as Maranhao and Bahia. The planners wanted the Goiana foco to be convenient to Brasilia, as a dramatization of the low defensive capability of the government.

University students were susceptible to the guerrilla recruiters' appeals, generally speaking more apt to be inspired by revolutionary rhetoric. However, they required some tangible outlet for their energies, not content merely to attend classes on tactics or plans for future campaigns. For the new recruits to the Goiana foco, generous funding of activities created a stirring of interest, but may have attracted ill-suited individuals who were overly romantic, or overly interested in the monetary inducements. They became indiscreet, bragging to friends and even taking unauthorized visitors to the camp on weekends. In time, even an incompetent army-police intelligence network could uncover the necessary information to prepare for a surprise raid, snuffing out the entire operation.

Concurrent investigations, especially following the crash of a Brazilian (Varig) airliner in Peru in November 1962 tied the president of the National Bank of Cuba and the Castro government to the guerrilla movement in central Brazil. Letters found on the person of Dr. Raul Cepero, the bank president, suggest strongly that Fidel Castro was the sponsor of the efforts, even while giving verbal support to the Goulart regime. Among the letters, there were complaints, expressed by Cuban supervisors of inefficiencies and corruption in the handling of funds given by Cuba for the use of organizers of the new guerrilla focos in Brazil. Particular mention was made of faults they found with actions by personnel attached to the Peasant League organization in the Northeast. It may well have been those discoveries that precipitated the rapid closing of the Dianapolis center in December, without waiting to entrap additional conspirators before May 1963 (Young 1972: 156).

Since it was believed, from various evidence collected, that the guerrilla foco would be heavily fortified, the matter was turned over to the Fourth Army, headquartered in Recife. It turned out that, although equipped with a sizable arms cache (which was captured, along with Morães and a few student guerrillas who were tried and imprisoned), the camp was not well defended due to lack of vigilance and poor guerrilla training. That experience, however, was certainly sufficient to alarm the army high command and to involve the staff of the Fourth Army, whose immediately preceding commander, Gen. Humberto Castello Branco, was by then the army chief of staff and, in a little more than a year, about to become president.

In an era dominated by concern over the spread of Castroism, Peasant League marches and plantation raids were also becoming an almost daily event reported in local presses. There is doubt that Julião's approval was sought for various peasant actions, which often led to his personal embarrassment—not so much for their militance as for their failures. On a typical occasion, in an attack on a plantation in Paraiba state, nineteen peasants were killed and many wounded when they were ambushed by armed militia forces (Page 1972: 184). Julião's movement seemed to be caught between the threat of being overtaken by competitor organizations if the League did not escalate its aggressiveness, and of being attacked by state and federal authorities in response to such activity.

It was also a time of impatience with legal methods. In his seminars at Cuernavaca, Julião pointed out (as I was later able to ascertain by other means) that the transistor radio had by the early 1960s become available to even very poor families in Brazil, and that peasant families often tuned in to hear Fidel Castro's nightly broadcasts from Radio Havana. By his excellent diction and impassioned rhetoric, even though given in Spanish rather than Portuguese, Castro's messages were not lost on the *Nordestino* peasant population. Night receptions were clear, even three thousand miles away, and audiences were always large.

The Northeastern Literacy Schools Movement

Just after the Cuban *Brigadista* volunteers had completed their yearlong campaign of 1961, an imitative operation was being launched in the rural areas of the Northeast. For some years, the state-supported Radio Schools of Literacy had been carrying out only slightly effective educational efforts. Whether the new wave of transistor radios was the spur, or the Cuban example, it appears that the two essential ingredients that could be added—on-scene instructors, and a new, appealing textbook—made a great difference after 1962. The text, *Vivere é Lutar*, and instruction techniques were developed at the state-funded Rural University of Pernambuco by Paulo Freire. Upon being popularized and widely propagated throughout the Northeast and other rural regions, this "Freire Method" drew the attention of public security officials for its alleged revolutionary agitation potential.

When Professor Freire came into the literacy extension and radio schools program, he found that the basic text and teaching style had little significance and negligible inspirational value to adults, so he set about devising materials and a new style of presentation that could greatly accelerate literacy education. As he explained it in his 1969 CIDOC seminar in Cuernavaca, it was only when the illiterate adults confronted socially stimulating topical material, slanted toward self-help and improved social opportunities, that they became aroused to take learning seriously. But even in the friendly environment at CIDOC, he declined to say whether he intended his book and techniques to arouse revolutionary discontent. Joseph Page (1972: 170–76), in conversations with some of Freire's former staff members, heard boasts that they could produce a "revolution in forty hours," but that may have been merely the repetition of their leader's claim that bringing about literacy through only forty hours of instruction was a revolutionary step in adult education. Whereas Freire had, at subsequent times, voiced opposition to guerrilla-imposed "liberations," there were many Freire staff workers personally convinced of the dire necessity for a mass-based, popular revolution (Lernoux 1982: 40).

Examination of the text, *Vivere é Lutar*, which was still in print at CIDOC but not within Brazil after the military coup, proved interesting, especially when I was later able to compare it with subsequent literacy texts in use in Pernambuco and Bahia in the 1970s. One could begin with the title: *To Live is to Fight*, or (as defenders of its innocuousness would assert), *To Live is to Struggle*. After exploring such themes as hunger, landlessness, and hard work, there were such lesson topics as: "Brazil needs to have a complete change," "How will Brazil be liberated from this situation?" "The people have a duty to fight for justice," "Let us go forth," and (concluding) "Continue until there is a change." Neale Pearson (1967: 154) reported, in interviewing the Fourth Army intelligence officer assigned to investigate the Freire system for adult education, that that officer concluded that revolutionary intent became so clear to him that it alone would have justified the 1964 military intervention. I too found subversive intent to be a significant ingredient in the textbook's presentation.

In a strategically important region with more than twice the population of Cuba, it is easy to see how the military authorities of Brazil felt more than a little concern over the possibilities of a revolutionary movement, signaled by the literacy and Peasant League organization efforts they were witnessing.

THE MILITARY RESPONSE TO REVOLUTIONARY AGITATION

Even though staff officers were aware of the poverty and the injustice they saw at close hand, especially in the Northeast, the natural reaction to alarm was to err on the side of increased security measures. They probably overreacted in closing down such programs as the Catholic Basic Education Movement (MEB), extension education and Radio Literacy Schools programs, and not only the *Ligas Campesinas* sponsored by Julião, but state-sponsored peasant unions as well. Then, operating from compiled lists of suspected subversives, army personnel rounded up leftist politicians and accused revolutionary leaders. These were dealt with, in drumhead trial fashion, by military police inquiries (IPMs) which handed out either imprisonments or, in many cases, official banishment from the country.

One of the most coveted postings for an army four-star general commander of one of Brazil's four field armies (or, perhaps an equivalent command of the Amazon forces), and those few generals will only have one such command. It seems more than coincidental that the first, second, and third generals chosen to be president each had been the Fourth Army commander, whose territory was the Northeast. There was significance in the perception that this was a prime target area for guerrilla activity, but by the time Ernesto Geisel was tapped as Medici's successor in 1974, the threat had subsided, and security measures were substantially relaxed. By the 1970s, when economic recovery measures had begun to show results, at least subduing the heretofore unparalleled economic chaos, attention turned to solving some of the social neglect.

Priority Attention to Reform Measures

The reforms closest to the hearts of the new government, purging the system of corrupt politicians and communists (as well as suspected fellow travelers), have been touched upon in connection with the discussion of the perceived Northeast threat; actually, the anticommunist sweep was nationwide, and it was an arbitrary, rapid operation. Next in importance came the immediate need to control and reduce the heretofore unprecedented inflation which gripped the country and caused economic depression at the level of the financial and mercantile elites. There was general recognition of the widespread misery afflicting the urban slums and rural inhabitants, but the prevailing economic doctrine of military leaders saw revitalization of the investment and fiscal climate as the key to subsequent improvement of levels of living among the Brazilian mass public. That doctrine originated primarily with the staff and students of the prestigious Escola Superior de Guerra (ESG), which is the topic of the next chapter.

Albert Fishlow (1973: 71–76) pointed out that the fiscal and economic policies of the first military government were based upon orthodox Western capitalist approaches to economic stabilization and inflation controls. The two chief components, which he was inclined to criticize, were to control demand-side spending and to encourage an influx of foreign investments based upon high-capital technology. Much of that came from the United States, accentuating the already dominant influence of the northern colossus and demoralizing—if not antagonizing—Brazilian industrial and financial entrepreneurs.

Though the Brazilian economy eventually flourished in the spectacular years of the "miraculous" growth rates of 10 percent annually, beginning several years after the coup, early results of the first and second military administrations widely discredited the leadership of the military as regarding the economy. The austerity prescribed by the government to encourage new investment funds, only widened the gap between the wealthy few and those barely at a subsistence level, while inflation remained no lower than 40 percent through the Castello Branco regime's three-year term.

Another reform prescribed on the basis of comparative studies at the ESG was to compress the multiparty political system into a two-party format, in order to make the presidential model of countries such as the United States more workable. Theoretically, the creation of a responsible, disciplined legislative majority should have improved executive-congressional relations, and in time should have produced a durable record of achievement which voters would respect and support. One could, for example, use long-lived and controversial issues such as enactment of land reforms as an illustration of past failures of government. Although past laws had been enacted with a flourish, creating expectations for the people who had supported politicians supposedly dedicated to the reform, almost no land reform had resulted, due to administrative refusal to vigorously execute laws that had been designed for demagoguery and easy obstruction. Another example was the creation of the Superintendency for Economic Development of the Northeast, most commonly known by the acronym SUDENE. Its primary role in the two brief years during Goulart's tenure as president had been to supplant patronage and graft dispensed in the drought works bureau (DNOCS) with yet another layer of bureaucracy; but the national politicians in Congress frustrated implementation of more effective reform measures by the new SUDENE staff. Military reforms might have turned this new structure into a vehicle for progress, assisted by generous support from the United States through its AID (Agency for International Development) and Alliance for Progress programs, but the purging of suspected communists and corrupt administrators inside SUDENE greatly curtailed its ability to produce development proposals and plans. Although SUDENE was generously funded, the purging of those with technical expertise at the implementing levels stalled activity at the planning and staffing stage.

Popularity of Technocratic Methods

As Gilbert Siegel (1973: 370) pointed out, centralized planning began with the Kubitschek government, achieving cabinet-level status under Goulart when he brought in Celso Furtado after launching SUDENE in the Northeast. Neither, however, proved capable of more than assembling a compact, national planning staff and an innocuous multiyear "plan" which could be approved by the Congress but did not have the teeth necessary to alter bureaucratic structures or the economic status quo. This administrative model appealed to the military hierarchy, who were disposed to rely upon bureaucratic approaches to problem solving.

After the Castello Branco regime took the reins in 1964, subtle but significant changes were made. Experts from the academic and business fields were not merely assembled to fill posts vacated after the purges, but were given unheard-of powers to effect changes in government-led reforms, for example, in revenue collection and public administration. Backed by a compliant rump Congress and an essentially apolitical leadership in Brasilia, a "state capitalist" regime manned by technocrats began what can best be described as government modeled after a planned economy.

Opinions differed among the observers of this emerging style of government. To dos Santos (1974: 464–80) and Dreifuss (1981: 419–55), the pattern and the results were proof of the intent to sell out Brazilian interests to American businessmen and financiers. Whereas Gilbert Siegel (1973: 372–75) believed the trend stemmed from intrinsic weakness due to critical shortages of qualified engineers and civil servants, Schmitter (1973: 205, 223–25) and Arrães (1972: 182–87) saw this as typical of the Latin or "Portugalized" corporatist method, abetting American interests. In my opinion, Skidmore (1973: 16–28) and Flynn (1979: 520) have come closest to correctly assessing what was behind the changed methods of administration. Beginning in the 1960s, with what was promised as a "peaceful revolution" under the Alliance for Progress program, controls and detailed, preplanned stages for use of capital investments became requisite to the release of the funds appropriated yearly, accompanied by accounting measures. What soon developed was necessarily arbitrary and undemocratic in appearance, but this aspect was not at the time criticized by a bureaucratic-minded military regime unaccustomed to taking very seriously the criticisms of disaffected businessmen and academic or journalistic critics. After all, this was to be a revolution, led by true patriots with only the nation's best interests at heart.

SUMMARY AND CONCLUSIONS

There is much to be said for the Huntington (1968) "political decay" thesis, put forth by Stepan (1978a) and Skidmore (1973) as the main factor in bringing civilian government under Goulart to a halt in 1964. His regime was in tatters, and he was attacked by even the most sympathetic of his critics as being weak (Galeano, 1964), ambivalent, and too undisciplined (Arrães 1972: 151–54). He was rash to the point of stupidity, as Stepan (1971 and 1978a), Schneider (1971), and Flynn (1979) agree, to have pushed the military to rebellion with no regard for the need to preserve hierarchy and a sense of discipline in the noncommissioned army and navy ranks.

Benefiting from hindsight and abundant, reliable sources, Stepan (1978a: 112) was led to believe that military and civil leaders in Brazil had worried excessively about the purported revolutionary threat in the Northeast. But if Goulart's incompetence, corruption within his inner circle, or even evidence of his intention to illegally extend his rule in the 1965 elections had been the basis of his removal, there would have been no salable pretext for the establishment of a long-term military rulership over Brazil. There may have been exaggeration in some quarters of the extent of the "communist threat" in the Northeast or elsewhere, but it was a time when even appearances of softness on communism would make civilian rule vulnerable to a military intervention.

If fear of subversive communism was a major factor in the forced removal of the Goulart regime—at cadre levels or beyond—as I contend, then the immediate availability of detailed and repeatedly reviewed plans developed at the ESG, by which to try out broad reform measures, was a major factor in giving military leaders the confidence that they could, together with a new group of apolitical expert staff members and sympathetic civilians from the political world, successfully introduce a whole range of measures to solve Brazil's many socioeconomic problems. Thus there was at least a temporary consensus within the military elite not only to intervene, but to embark upon a lengthy period of direct control over the policy-making process. To be sure, the prospect of taking power for themselves was appealing for its promise of various rewards, including both money and authority. Even so, there was a fundamental sense of mission—of not merely rescue but redirection toward a better future for the country—in the minds of the military elite, down to the level of most of the career officer corps. Since the perceived wise guidance of studies on assorted problems produced by the Escola Superior de Guerra was so closely related to the spirit and ideologic thought of those leaders in the 1960s (and thereafter), we turn next to an analysis of the role of the ESG in that undertaking by Brazil's military elite.

2

The Political Influence of the Escola Superior de Guerra

Through differing perspectives, some consensus apparently has emerged concerning the crucial role that Brazil's Escola Superior de Guerra played in the military governments. The ESG, to use its identifying acronym rather than adherents' favorite sobriquet of "Sorbonne," seems at the very least to have popularized within both civilian and military elites the conviction that Brazil's anticipated future as a major world power (*grandeza*) might be achieved by use of the intellectual contributions of the school. Because the ESG is so widely recognized as the major contributor to the "mission" which the military leadership adopted in 1964, and because it continued to attract ministerial-level attention to its studies and its ideological guidance, an in-depth study seems important.

Scholars of the Brazilian political system in the postwar era have seen the Escola Superior de Guerra as the proponent of military role expansion into formerly acknowledged civilian domains, variously perceived as fostering "new professionalism" (Stepan 1973: 47–65), "antipolitics" (Loveman and Davies 1978: 11), "patrimonialism" (Roett 1972: 102), or as a vehicle for "cooptation" of important civil sectors (Schneider 1971: 250). At the outset, it is important to recognize that there were important differences between the ideology expressed through scholarship and lectures at the ESG and what was being voiced by other Brazilian centers of political and developmental ideology. To cite Alfred Stepan, "The most influential school of development ideology in Brazil in the 1950s, the Brazilian Institute for Socioecomic Studies (ISEB) emphasized nationalism and the public sector. The ESG, however, influenced by its FEB (Brazilian Expeditionary Force) experience, cared more about efficiency and productivity . . . " (1971: 245). Stepan points out that there was a less nationalistic flavor to ESG philosophy, presumed to stem from an unconcealed admiration for the United States, its government, economic prowess, international policy orientation in its senior military institutions, and enthusiasm for the concepts behind post–World War II creation of its National War College. Yet, unlike attitudes commonly associated with the ESG's North American mentors, Brazil's senior military institution came to display disdain for the civil leadership, which received much of the blame for the nation's present underdeveloped state. Some background on the creation and initial orientation of the ESG is provided here, for a better understanding of fundamental ways in which it has differed from similar institutions in the developed world. Other sources to consult include Stepan (1971: 172–87); Roett (1972: 102–4); and Arruda (1983), extensively quoted below.

BACKGROUND OF THE FOUNDING OF THE ESCOLA SUPERIOR DE GUERRA

One of the first deliberate actions taken by the United States, following the conclusion of World War II, was to attempt unification of the armed forces, and preparation of senior military leaders at military war colleges through post-graduate studies, for future roles in national strategic planning. Chiefs of staff of the four armed services (army, navy, marine corps, and the new air force) were to be joined by a senior officer as chairman of the "Joint Chiefs of Staff." They were to be further combined within a secretary of defense superstructure and, to institutionalize military collaboration under these changes, the National War College was also created to inculcate the new spirit of unity. These reorganizing actions preceded by only a few years quite similar measures within Brazil's military establishment. By 1949, it too had a National Security Council, an Armed Forces General Staff headed by a cabinet-level officer and—using guidance from a special mission drawn from staff members of the new U.S. National War College,—the Escola Superior de Guerra as a "capstone" leadership producer.

Although the two senior institutions of military strategic study no longer bear great similarity, the pattern of military restructuring which took place almost simultaneously in both nations was not merely coincidental. Without doubt they were directly linked to the experiences of Brazil's FEB (Brazilian Expeditionary Force) during World War II. To a lesser degree, they were associable with the Brazilian navy's losses and its costly lessons in modern warfare received during its patroling operations in the Atlantic during the war. Uniquely among the Latin American nations, all but one of which had declared war with the Axis following the U.S. entry as a belligerent, Brazil had deployed a division abroad to fight alongside the U.S. Army. It initially suffered heavy losses, but managed after some delay to distinguish itself, during hard fighting in central Italy, by defeating well-trained German forces and seizing Monte Cassini pass.

Unlike the Brazilian navy, which had since 1922 received assistance and training from a U.S. naval mission and had its own Naval War College, the army had found itself in need of better instruction, logistic and leadership reorganization, and equipment modernization. Stepan (1971: 87, 239–44) carefully documented how the Brazilian army's postwar leadership emerged from those wartime experiences with a strong pro-American bias, based not only upon personal comradeship but also upon admiration of their Yankee mentors' methods and organization. Further, these Brazilian war veterans, just like Americans, returned home after the war with fresh resolve to attempt changes they believed necessary to amend former ways of life in the Brazilian society.

Creation of the new graduate level professional school for senior officers seemed to lay groundwork for the effective unifying of efforts of the armed forces through closer association. Until then, with the army enjoying unquestioned dominance in matters of policy and fiscal support, there had been little basis for any cooperation. In fact, competition for scarce resources had only drawn the services further apart. In the mid–1950s, the Brazilian navy and air force had nearly come to blows over the issue of which service would operate helicopters from the newly acquired light aircraft carrier *Minas Gerais*. It took army intervention on the side of the air force, along with the influence of politicians tending to line up in opposition to the more patrician navy, to resolve that dispute. Thus, earnest efforts were made in the ESG to create coequal status for each of the three services. Inclusion of senior naval officers as teammates for a year with army and air force officers of similar rank was important in bridging such disputes as the navy–air force wrangle over which service should operate from the carrier.

Though the recent war experience changed personal philosophies, it did not alter such traditions as the giving of a name to the new school. Brazil's original Escola Superior de Guerra, operated from 1942 to 1944, was created for the preparation of generals, and for colonels about to pin on the star, to assume roles in the army's High Command. It came to an abrupt end with the sending of Brazil's FEB to Italy, as staffing requirements stripped the school of both staff and students. When consciousness of the new purpose of the second ESG became widespread, there were several proposals to change the name in favor of non-belligerent-sounding appellations such as "Institute for Studies of National Security," or "School for Study of Defense," each time however lacking high-level support. The school's designated historian and long-term faculty member, Antonio de Arruda (1983: xxii) records that the founders of the new institution considered it "inadvisable to pattern itself after the U.S. National War College," since Brazil's needs were to develop elites for solving peacetime problems. For example, he cites the first ESG commandant, Marshal Oswaldo Cordeiro de Farias, at the ceremonies commemorating ESG's twenty-fifth anniversary, who said "The ESG is a daughter of the Americans, but it has naturalized itself Brazilian" (1983: xxxviii). Each national institution has evolved, but Brazil's ESG seems more fully transformed by the course of world affairs. Evidence of its departure from the American model can be detected by examining the founders' initial conceptions.

Fundamental Founding Principles

One of the initial lecturers at the ESG, Lt. Col. Idalio Sardenberg (subsequently a general), is credited with enunciating with the seven guiding principles, which still endure (de Arruda 1983: xxii):

1. National security is a function of the overall power—rather than the military power—of the nation.
2. Brazil has the basic requisites—area, population, and resources—essential to become a major world power.
3. Brazil's national development has been retarded by factors susceptible to change.
4. As in all forms of work, development will necessitate the use of a mobilizing energy, and the application of that energy.
5. Until now, the obstacles to national solutions to Brazil's problems have been deficient processes adopted for application of this energy, and an absence of habits of working together.
6. Urgent replacement of a "method of opinions" by other methods will produce more balanced and harmonious solutions.
7. The instrument to be utilized for adoption and dissemination of a new method consists in the creation of a national institute of graduate-level study which should also function as a permanent research center.

Sardenberg's "Institute" would depend far more upon human than natural factors for its success, above all by capacitating various leaders to work together in sustained efforts uncharacteristic of past patterns of work. He conceived of the following style for future ESG studies:

1. A National Strategic Concept produced through analysis and interpretation of economic, political, diplomatic, and military factors;
2. An environment of broad understanding among groups representing these four official functions, accustomed to interdepartmental collaboration and working closely together;

3. Broad, objective conceptions of National Security which serve as a base for coordinating actions of every agency, civil or military, having responsibilities related to national power and security.

New Concept of War. The conventional wisdom at the time Brazil sent forces to fight with the Allies in World War II held that war-making must be left to generals. With the new knowledge gained about a "total war," however, the ESG saw future engagements differently. Equipment, air support, logistics, and particularly strategic and tactical concepts had to change when faced with the prospect of urban devastation on a scale previously unimagined. Perhaps most of all, the FEB soldiers and airmen gained new admiration for the Allied nations' organizational behavior and their strong sense of morale—attributable, they believed, to norms of democratic social order prevalent in their countries, contrasting markedly with the fascist systems of the Germans and Italians. Finally, they came to recognize that national power, made evident on battlefields and in task forces at sea, depended so much on industrial might.

Brazil's foreign policy alignment with the West had hardly been questioned until 1960, lagging by a decade the global shift of strategy from that of future "total wars" to the reality of Cold War between the two superpowers and their satellite nations. When the change of perspective came, an immediate consequence was greater concern for national security as it related to interests and policy issues, and much less consideration of comparative strengths of fighting forces in relation to those of potential opponents. In Brazil, to a much greater degree than in the United States and its NATO allies, the perception of Cold War conflict tended to embrace such broad aspects as moral values and the need to fortify those institutions that preserved national values (de Arruda 1983: xxiv). It should be recalled that until the 1960s the Catholic tradition and the Church's status in Brazil were so monolithic and influential that such issues as divorce, birth control, abortion, or celibacy in the priesthood were not viewed as being open to debate.

Structure of the School. As in any institution of higher learning, founders of the ESG necessarily distinguished between students and members of its faculty and staff. Evidently intending to impart greater collegial spirit, the latter were labelled *Corpo Permanente* (permanent staff)—actually, in the case of military members, toured for three or four years—while its student body received the name of *Corpo de Estagiaros,* an unfamiliar term with implications of "in-service trainees" but perhaps meant to merely indicate the annual flow of matriculants. The presiding senior official, titled *Comandante,* was usually a four-star army general, though occasionally the post was given to a similarly ranked naval or air force officer. In deference to service equality, the *Subcomandante* was drawn from another service, at the three-star rank, and each of the three service branches was further represented by another, two-star member with the title of Assistant Commandant, bearing specific responsibility as a "course director," (to be further delineated below). The permanent staff also included ministers, second class, from the foreign relations ministry, from the justice ministry, and perhaps one or two other ministries. The remainder of the permanent staff was about evenly divided between senior level members of the three armed forces and civilians, titled "professors." For this assignment, they were frequently drawn from government agencies and ministries, rather than from major universities.

The Senior Course at the ESG was the feature attraction in terms of national security policy-making, and it was the principal course that enrolled the selected mix of military and civilian students. In addition to the CSG (Curso Superior de Guerra) or Senior Course, as we shall term it and study it here, there was a course in Major Command and Staff of the Armed Forces (CEMCFA) which ran nine months concurrently. It occasionally merged with the Senior Course, and only enrolled military officers. Originally, there were also two shorter (discontinued) courses: National Mobilization, which dealt with industrial planning, and Information, which dealt with intelligence and counterintelligence affairs. After the government established a new School of Information in Brasilia, the Information Course at the ESG was terminated in 1973. Concurrently, the scope and base of the SNI (National Intelligence Service) mushroomed and soon came to be one of the more serious threats to the president's control over the bureaucracy and armed services.

Extension activities of the ESG were a minor undertaking, represented by a correspondence course and an "Updating" Course for alumni who wished to keep themselves more current than the larger numbers of alumni who attended the weekly or monthly club-like luncheons and social events of the very large ADESG (Alumni Association).

Student Selection in the Senior Course. Whereas there are five military students for each civilian (government official) student at the U.S. National War College, in Brazil there are often more civilian than military students. Often the numbers who are not employed in government agencies nearly equals the size of the civilian bureaucracy, and either category may equal the numbers coming from active military duty.

Military enrollments are under the control of the three service ministries, pursuant to quotas and nominal approval from the EMFA (Armed Forces General Staff), as the ministerial level senior of the ESG Commandant. Civilians coming to the Senior Course from government service are also "quotaed" by the EMFA and approved, first by the responsible ministry or government corporation, then by the EMFA staff. Nongovernment civilians gain entry by application—as often recruited as they are self-initiated—and have varied in numbers, constituting what may be seen as a barometer of the political environment in Brazil. I learned from staff members of the ESG that the usual procedure is to screen out twice as many from the so-called "cooptive sector" as they accept for enrollment in the Senior Course. Applicants (and military and government nominees) must be between ages 35 and 55, and aside from clearances from the SNI and service bureaucracies, the selection process emphasizes candidates' academic credentials and other scholarly attainments. Those with bachelor's degrees have perhaps a one in three chance of acceptance, about two out of three at the master's level are taken, and possession of a doctorate degree almost assures acceptance. Brazil did not break the gender barrier until 1973 when two female students were enrolled, enlarging to four the following year, and leveling out at eight per class since 1980. Their numbers have been kept even for convenience in assignments to apartments in the nearby impressive high-rise building which is provided to students without Rio residences by the government.

Alumni Association. In evident appreciation of the importance for Brazil's further progress and political direction, and probably also in recognition of the odds against bringing to fruition any plans or policies conceived during the nine-month course, the graduates of the first two years' classes founded an alumni organization in Rio de Janeiro to maintain contact with colleagues, and to foster useful networks among their clan. In ensuing years, every state capital and a few other urban centers joined the ADESG (Associação dos Diplomados da Escola Superior de Guerra) organization, meeting monthly or as often as weekly to continue their relationships with fellow alumni and with the school. Besides the luncheons and social events of these "clubs," the Alumni Association soon saw that their slender ranks would hardly sustain viable presences as vehicles for influence, and therefore initiated their own abbreviated versions of the Senior Course in 1953. By the 1980s, more than 90 percent of the ADESG membership comprised graduates of the four-month Cycles of Studies courses, available in eighteen "Ciclos" study centers scattered throughout Brazil. More than a thousand new members of ADESG are added annually to the roll, which numbers well over forty thousand by now.

The content of these ADESG cycles is monitored closely by the parent organization in Rio, and the ESG provides some of its own permanent staff as lecturers for initial and closing portions of the cycles at each location. The Alumni Association depends heavily upon the school to be "the generator of ideas," while ADESG serves as the means of broadly spreading its core concepts (ADESG[n.d.]: 6). While we have no impartial basis to compare the ESG alumni and their profit from the nine-month course to those who complete ADESG's Cycles, it is clear that the latter must have substantial personal interest in the program to be willing to commit themselves to nightly meetings of several hours' length, and considerable outside work as well. Additionally, each ADESG enrollee must pay a sum of as much as $200 (U.S. dollars), in monthly installments of about $50 (two times the regional minimum wage) in Rio or São Paulo. Proportionately smaller rates apply to less prosperous areas, where salaries of professionals also are lower (ADESG 1984: 13).

Instructional Methods. Whereas the major productive effort on the part of Senior Course students actually derives from what are called *Trabalhos de Equipe* (Team Studies), most of the reputation and prestige attached to the ESG has come as a result of extensive media attention given to policy declarations and program outlines presented to the class by government leaders in Congress, the ministries, and other high offices. As one of the staff members confided to me, the true value of these "big shows" in comparison to other aspects of a course varies in inverse proportion to the national attention it receives.

Team studies are organized near the outset of the course, following four weeks of what is described as "doctrinal study." The ESG *Basic Manual* outlines five stages of the team study: preparation (self-study of material provided), research (extending for many subsequent weeks), discussions (led by a staff member or an appointed student study director), elaboration (the drafting and finished writing efforts), and finally, the team report (published and presented to all students in assembly).

Some team reports have received top-level attention, and have led to program initiations or policy changes. Falling into predetermined topical areas, each deals with some protracted national or regional problem purportedly threatening national security. In a typical year, these are apt to be topics undertaken for team studies: Amazonian policy and ecological consequences, Antarctic exploration and national geostrategic rights, communication policy and psychosociology, alcohol fuel substitution and national energy policy, demographics and birth control, drugs and youth issues, education policy and national development, drought and Northeast development, housing policy and urban development, feminism and social policy, health and public services, interiorization and colonization policy, and international trade and technology exchange agreements (de Arruda, 1983: 87–88; ADESG, 1984: 5–6). Some team studies regularly enjoy ministry sponsorship and budgetary support, and most reports are circulated and further debated within agencies and ministries. Each class also takes study trips—all groups, rather than just the group preparing a team study report—to areas many have not previously seen, including the Amazonian territories bordering neighbor nations, and lesser-studied areas of the Northeast. In the years prior to the debt crisis, whole classes regularly spent a week or more on an extended study trip to the United States, marking that as a highlight of the Senior Course.

A few students who are recognized at the outset for special expertise have been given individual, "special studies" projects. When high-level interest or past achievements from team studies may warrant, a few students may be grouped with invited national experts and a staff member to prepare a major planning study report (*Trabalho de Planejamento*). Such reports ordinarily take their policy cues from past studies or current decree laws, and then attempt to lay out comprehensive plans for government action to accomplish the program. Naturally, those who have been singled out for such studies—as above, carried out in the group study fashion—have been identified for their past work and experience in analysis of alternative methods, feasibility and cost estimates, and public administration skills. If the planning study results are deemed worthy (i.e., major questions have been debated to general agreement), the team makes a plenary presentation to the whole class, and may be subsequently sent to Brasilia or to other locales to attempt to "sell" the plans.

It can be seen from this discussion that the ESG believes itself fully capable of advising governmental leaders on policy questions affecting security and development.

THE DOCTRINE OF NATIONAL SECURITY

Unquestionably, the "doctrine" and the Law of National Security have been objects of contention, often cited as the justification for human rights abuses by the state. Even defenders argue that repression of the political opposition takes place in pursuit of asserted, higher state priorities. More often than not, accusers have identified the ESG as the leader in the enunciation and amendments of the "doctrine of national security." Ample evidence could be provided to support my contention that, even in its most authoritarian period, Brazil was much less an offender of human rights than comparable regimes, internationally or within the hemisphere. The following analysis of the doctrine considers first what it professes, how it has influenced political processes, criticisms and defenses of the doctrine, and finally, the extent to which it has affected policy-making and politics since 1964.

Content of the National Security Doctrine

The ESG contends that its "doctrine" is not presented as a dogma, but it holds certain specified "national interests" to be immutable. The doctrine needs regular revisions to adapt to a changing environment, but a key tenet is that Brazil's national security is linked indefinitely to national development. The second commandant, Juarez Távora (1953: 9) was the first to utter this principle, which has been often reiterated. President Castello Branco (1967: 3), at the end of his term, again stated this principle, which remains firmly held. The doctrine is seen as a product, assembled and packaged by the ESG, then marketed through proclamations and high officials' speeches to political elites, who may also have attended the Senior Course and consider it the most valid interpreter of the statuses of security and development.

Basic Definitions. In its early years, the definition of "national security" given by Juarez Távora, generally accepted and used for many years, was "the pursuit and safeguarding of its national objectives against adverse internal or external factors" (Távora 1953: 7). By 1983, usage had revised the definition, as given in the ESG *Basic Manual* (1983: 206), to: "The guarantee by the state in particular, to the degree feasible, for the benefit of the Nation, by means of political, economic, psychosocial and military actions, of secured and maintained Permanent National Objectives, in spite of existing or potential antagonisms and pressures."

Literature emanating from the ESG to define the Permanent National Objectives over three decades, while voluminous, can be reduced in the essence to such well-known—and thus not too revealing—valued objects as national unity, independence, full employment and well-being, appreciation of human values, health, democracy, international respect, and social peace (de Arruda 1983: 77–83). Controversy enters in attempts to define such less value-free concepts as the "Common Good." It centers around such issues as the preference for advancing comprehensive development objectives, indefinitely postponing the distribution of past economic gains, or attempting minimally to reduce Brazil's very wide gap between the few wealthy and the multitude that have scarcely felt any relief of their poverty. It has always been a firm belief at the ESG that distribution must not begin until the country has attained those higher national objectives which fall into the "future greatness" category.

Since ESG places so much emphasis on national policy-making and governmental leadership, we need to examine how the "state" was perceived. Citing from a lecture of his own given in 1971, Arruda (1983: 149) gives this definition: "The *State* is the sovereign entity of a political nature, established within a determined territory, seeking to promote the conquest and the maintenance of the National Objectives of a people, within the criterion of the Common Good." For the hardliner faction, only a short conceptual leap was necessary to see antagonism against the government's policies—even pressures for income redistribution—as opposition which must be suppressed on behalf of higher state objectives—that is, the "common good." In this manner, authority was assumed to establish "National Interests," a "National Policy," and the "National Strategy" by which obstacles to the attainment of the "Permanent National Interests" were to be overcome (ESG *Basic Manual* 1983: 43–44, 97, 109).

Viewpoint Toward Opposition. Key words in doctrinal statements—such as "obstacles," "antagonisms," and "pressures," all designating what had to be resisted or overcome—are important ideological clues. The terms have been debated for years in the ESG with mixed reactions. A typical treatment, though it may appear to be just hair-splitting, consisted of identifying a fundamental distinction between broad varieties of oppositional activities and those actions categorized by the ESG as "active contesting with the leadership for control." Ordinary opposing actions included all those accepted, familiar freedoms open to any rival group or individual in a democracy. Active contesting, on the contrary, was deemed to have crossed over the line of permissable actions available to oppose a government.

The above concepts posed an interesting dilemma. What should be the judgment concerning the actions taken in the 1964 coup? Narrow and convoluted logic was brought to bear, tending toward silence regarding the existence of active plotting against Goulart within the military elite, and concluding that the president had lost a legitimate right to rule through his departure from the seat of government unto unknown, unavailable whereabouts—his ranch in the southernmost state of Rio Grande do Sul—at a time when the existing crisis required his presence in Brasilia. It was also noted that, in leaving the country for exile in Uruguay, the president failed to meet the constitutional requirement that he obtain the consent of Congress to do so. For the ESG, niceties of legitimacy required a legalistic form of argument. Of course, most of the military elite appeared to regard the president as illegitimate for their own reasons, beginning either when he entered the office of president or when he made proclamations tantamount to declaring himself a revolutionary.

A standard approach regarding the legitimacy of an opposition was to differentiate between resistance to "present governmental objectives" and the ethereal standard of "permanent national objectives." The ESG, not being required to specify more than generally what was illegitimate, resorted to a most exalted level of authority: the pope! Arruda (1983: 52) in this connection cited the 1967 Papal Encyclical *Populorum Progressio* of Paul VI to the effect that "unreasonable contestations" amounted to acts which threaten liberty itself by corrupting human spirits, *or by provoking repression in response to such contestations*. In the unfolding era of guerrilla and counterguerrilla operations, it had become clear that narrow concepts of national strategy formerly limited to external war and war readiness in peacetime, enunciated by Golbery (do Couto e Silva 1954: 14) and others, now required much broader definition. Doing this produced a divisive issue: a minority inclined toward totalitarian reaction, but many viewpoints competed over boundary placement in suppressing the opposition. Did the "doctrine" truly *require* repression?

Critical Views of the Doctrine, and Rebuttals

Among the principal condemnations of Brazil's Doctrine of National Security, the most familiar viewpoint was that it was based upon a power elite mentality that was quite antidemocratic. Some critics charged the doctrine with being overly ambitious and self-aggrandizing, in that it greatly expanded the scope of matters falling within the military purview. Others charged it with elitism and exclusivism, with being overly bureaucratic, or with lacking true national authenticity, either by its pro-Western tilt or by an anticommunism that was blinded to the many ways in which Brazilian society had failed its poverty-level majority. One finds all these themes in two works that concentrated most directly on the subject: Joseph Comblin's *The Ideology of National Security,* and Brian Loveman and Thomas E. Davies's *The Politics of Antipolitics.*

My survey of the literature, in addition to those two works, attempts to balance external and Brazilian viewpoints. For the latter, principal comments to follow came from Fernando Henrique Cardoso (alone and with coauthor Enzo Faletto) in the 1970–1972 period, Miguel Arrães in the 1969–1972 period, Celso Furtado in the late 1960s, Candido Mendes in the 1966–1972 era, and Rene Dreifuss (Uruguayan, but also now Brazilian) in the late 1960s and early 1970s. Among the outsiders, principal criticisms have come from Jan K. Black, Peter Flynn, Peter McDonough, Philippe Schmitter, Ronald Schneider, Thomas Skidmore, and Alfred Stepan. All of the above works were begun more than a decade ago, and each has been well received and critiqued in the United States and abroad. Since more recent social science literature concerning Brazil reveals quite different impressions following the liberalization trend of the mid–1970s, it seems important—especially in the case of authors living in Brazil in the late 1960s to early 1970s of greatest repressions—to state when the authors penned their comments.

Antidemocratic Values. Even before the new constitution of 1967, embodying among other things the Law of National Security, was publicly available in draft, Candido Mendes (1966) had sized up the Castello Branco regime and its uncontested successor, Costa e Silva, as being of the power elite variety. He saw the first military regime as a "modernizing autocracy" of civilian as well as military men drawn from the ESG, armed with their National Security Doctrine and determined to avoid any personal ties to power-wielding, seeking thereby to avoid the trappings of a "formalized dictatorship." The successor regime, as Mendes viewed it, was able to profit from the lead given it in better personnel and policies, but it more ruthlessly drove for ruling power, abandoning self-imposed democratic restraints that had been observed in the Castello Branco government. Fernando Cardoso (1973: 165–67) suggested that Mendes may have ingenuously accepted the stated aims and political platforms of the first government's policy-makers as durable commitments. As a result, the Mendes power elite model required some "irreconcilable ad hoc reinterpretations" that often departed from his initial construct, "evolving into a thinly disguised normative view."

Philippe Schmitter (1973: 218–19), writing concurrently, labeled the doctrine "impeccably authoritarian," and suggestive of a durable dictatorship of the Salazar-Caetano variety: his "Portugalization" thesis. He implied that, in the wake of the 1964 coup, the doctrine may have been considered a convenient facade, useful to institutionalize the regime by mass indoctrination aimed at producing a subject-type political culture.

In retrospect, that judgment now seems rash and rancorous. Even Padre Joseph Comblin (1980: 160–64), despite his strong antipathy for the National Security Doctrine and the security state that it had inspired, made extensive allowance for the dominating influence of the non-ESG "hardline element" which, despite being a minority group, held a controlling leash on policy decisions. Many qualified judgments, such as that of Thomas E. Skidmore (1973: 5–17), could be cited to support Comblin's assessment of the strength of the hard-liners' political influence. Still, we are left with the question of whether oft-repeated democratic rhetoric was hollow, or merely unrealistic while genuine in intent. Each hypothesis has its adherents and its plausible arguments.

Elitism, Exclusivism, and Bureaucratism. Each of the first three military governments relied extensively upon studies of the ESG for the flesh of their ambitious-sounding national development plans. Though much of the Castello Branco term was spent in purging and reclaiming economic momentum, before 1967 the department under Planning Secretary Roberto Campos had its *Plano Deçenal* (for the 1970s) and *Projeto 2001* (Twenty-first Century!) in print. The latter was quickly touched up and renamed *Projeto Brasil* when the Costa e Silva team took over, and barely three years later, the Medici regime—installed with few replacements in the wake of Costa e Silva's fatal stroke—issued its *Mêtas e Bases Para a Ação do Govêrno* (Goals and Foundations for Government Action). Each was bureaucratic and frankly unrealistic, in that none of them had a firm basis of economic projections or, much more significantly, an effective lower-level echelon of administrators. They only had upper-and mid-level bureaucrats whose ideas bore strong ties to the ESG and its alumni.

Elitism and bureaucratism, often raised as criticisms of government with which one's personal objectives differ, are familiar to most governing systems. Thus, to Dreifuss (1981: 77–82), the National Security Doctrine and the elite network of the ESG represented a "conquest of the State by foreigners," made more possible by the flaws in the plan's foundations. In the same vein, Hêlio Jaguaribe (1968: 33–34) saw the extent to which Brazilian economic investment opportunities were opened up to multinational (especially American) corporations as "colonial fascism." Those sins were traced to the ESG and its Doctrine, but also to excessively narrow administrative practices.

A second administrative fault, as viewed by critics, was the dependence upon an all-powerful center which in turn relied upon a small coercive arm, and loose cooptive control over the entrepreneurial class members, seen by Cardoso (1973: 172–76) as being in league with "associated" (i.e., external investor) interests. Candido Mendes (1969: 70) points out the consequences for power and effectiveness of past regimes' insulation from the public. Similar criticisms of exclusiveness and elitism appear in Mendes (1977: 78–79), McDonough (1981: 99–106), Comblin (1980: 161), and Schmitter (1973: 218). They also cite as a third basis for criticism the regimes' tendency to count only economic gains as the criterion for program aims, and for execution of such plans. According to Schmitter (1973: 218), "It is too rigid in fixing system goals, and hence, it may be incompatible with the goals of economic, social and religious elites . . ."

Celso Furtado (1968: 7–23) cites this narrow elitism as a factor in favoring agrarian-financial interests above the other elements of Brazil's society. This "pastoralization," as he has labeled the policy, created stagnation since only the agrarian economic sector remained open to absorb unemployment. As in much of the criticisms being considered, these comments derive from the first few policy initiatives under Castello Branco—whose government faced the task of forcing a downward inflationary spiral through economic austerity—with an inevitable effect of creating lingering, unfavorable feelings toward the following regimes, despite their differences. Accusations of a rigid mindset may have applied as accurately to those voicing the criticisms.

Excessively Ambitious and Unrealistic. Typical of other views would be this summation by Joseph Comblin (1980: 159–60): That the military regimes, while repeating assurances of their desire to return to democratic forms, "more as an official rite than as genuine intention," assumed that institutions such as the Congress, when removed from effective power, may sustain the appearance of real dialogue and consultation on decisions by the executive powers. His best example was Costa e Silva's pledge to "humanize his government" with such actions as instituting consultations with representatives of the labor and student movements, while at the same time abolishing their opportunities for freedom of action under the 1967 Constitution and reacting in anger when he was rebuffed.

Others such as Dreifuss (1981: 361, 364–73) and Stepan (1973: 56–59; and 1978a: 120) tended, with different perspectives as to the motives of the elites, to see new directions taken under military regimes as having stemmed from the ambition for more power in the pursuit of state objectives. Their differences lie in their perception of the need for improvement of the national development efforts, rather than in the satisfaction of personal ambitions. However, they reached the same conclusions: too much concentration of power in the hands of inexperienced military executives; excessive role expansion, aggravated by faulty assessment of the ability of a narrow civil and military elite to engender support; and the absence of proper lower-level supervision of ambitious national development plans that deviated significantly from patterns of the past. Improved professional public administration was an unquestionable need, recognized too late in the rush toward execution of these plans.

Cardoso's criticisms (1973: 158–63) of military governments focused more narrowly on the direction adopted for economic strategy under the Doctrine. It was folly, he believed, to try to make the greatly enlarged state apparatus more productive—emphasizing a strong executive, broadened powers for the National Security Council, a new intelligence service (SNI), and tighter linkages between planning and executive agencies—while changing from a nationally centered to an internationalized bourgeoisie. The situation was not made better by increased repressive measures when the policy changes encountered resistance, with the inevitable charge that the government had sold out to foreign interests.

Antinationalist Policies. The earliest policy moves that were taken in the Castello Branco government showed a recognized tilt in the direction of the West, especially toward the United States. Inevitably, there were sharp criticisms of this aspect of the National Security Doctrine for its reliance upon foreign supporters and the consequent loss of nationalist autonomy. Some critics saw such policy directions as "imperialism" (Arrães 1972: 169–95), *entreguismo* (i.e., the "selling out" of Brazil's interests to foreigners) at official levels of government policy (Dreifuss 1981: 74–80), the cooptation of military leadership away from the popular "third option" politics of the Kubitschek-Quadros-Goulart era by American mentors (Skidmore 1967: 330), or uncritical, inauthentic imitation of American economic and political doctrines (Comblin 1980: 151–55). These charges were all to be found in the broadside attack by Jan Knippers Black (1977) in her *United States Penetration of Brazil*, and in similarly oriented works by Phylis Parker and Hêlio Jaguaribe.

A similar argument could be made about the concentration of authority, under the revised constitution, and its fundamental doctrine in the hands of non-elected officials of the civilian and military elite. What was at stake was the contention that an elite with no linkage to popular sectors through party-based patronage or clientele support, as in former times when Congress had its normal influence, was perforce without nationalistic roots, in terms of responsiveness to the collective national will. But Riordan Roett (1972: 176 and passim) persuasively argued that no such linkage with the "popular will" has ever existed within Brazil, nor was there ever a well-established or significant role for the legislative body in what was supposedly a democracy. His argument applies also to policy-making at the state level, through extension, because even state governors derived more of their effectiveness through linkages with the national party system and federal bureaucracies than through responsiveness to local popular pressures. Candido Mendes (1977: 20–24) draws much the same conclusion about pre–1964 populist governments.

Rebuttal of Foregoing Criticisms. It would be logical to expect little defense of the role of the National Security Doctrine to emerge from writings by Brazil's opposition, most of whom came from the intelligentsia. However, that is not the case, as may be seen from extracts of critical essays by Cardoso, Arrães, and even Comblin. The latter, while making severe criticisms of effects of policies emanating from the National Security Doctrine, generously credits Brazil's military elite with high, ostensibly democratic intentions (1980: 159–62). He specifically points to the difference between the ESG policy line which dominated the first regime's decisions and a small but potent hard-line element which was not in sympathy with the ESG doctrine. Note also what Cardoso (1973: 158) says concerning the first military regime:

> The government clearly intended to abide by its promise to restore democratic forms after purging the populist element. An illustration of this intent was Castello Branco's pledge to respect the electoral calendar, despite the risks this might imply for the regime.

Miguel Arrães (1972: 188), who like Cardoso remained active in the present political opposition after 1985, saw the military in quite similar terms:

> The imperialists are divided into "hard-line" elements and moderates. Their chief policy-making and propaganda centre is at the Higher School of Warfare[literal translation of Escola Superior de Guerra] known as the "Sorbonne." After Marshal Castello Branco's death, the moderates joined forces with the political groups working for the liberalization of the regime and the return of democracy to the country, though without seeking in any way to upset the political system established before April, 1964.

Alexandre de S. C. Barros (1985: 72) points out that various senior military men, most notably the navy minister, despite the reasonable fears of a postliberalization backlash—the "Argentine Factor," alluding to the criminal trials and incarcerations of senior military men in Brazil's southern neighbor—publicly stated their conviction that Brazil should then yield to the pressures of the massive *Diretas já* movement by holding direct presidential elections, rather than the controlled, indirect balloting for the first civilian president, as was done in 1985.

No intent exists here to rebut the common notion that the military governments were elitist and highly bureaucratic. It is important, however, to insert information opposing stereotypical versions of how the regimes were directed, coming from better-informed native sources. Few outsiders nor even many members of the civilian elite at the time knew of the extent to which the military organizations were safeguarded from the kind of encrusted autocracies of old, or of Chile or Paraguay in the same period. The best authority available would without doubt be Alexandre Barros, who served on the ESG permanent faculty, and whose dissertation for his doctorate from the University of Chicago was by far the most extensive research on the Brazilian military institution thus far attempted. In an interesting footnote, Barros (1985: 72) drew attention to such precautionary measures (not often found in Latin American states) as requiring military officers to limit service in a civilian administrative capacity to no more than two years, after which they would either resign their commission or return to normal military assignments. Thus would the likelihood of a "military-industrial complex" be greatly reduced. Similarly, the president and any of his appointees to ministries or high positions, except to the traditional posts as ministers of the army, navy, air force, and armed forces general staff, were also required to retire, and thereafter never appeared in uniform.

Since influence in the service hierarchy depends as much on the officer's future as on his present status, these rules made creation of a military "iron guard" most unlikely. Elitism and bureaucratic mentalities were probably as dominant during the military rulerships as in prior and subsequent years, but the risks of falling into the pattern of Paraguay's Stroessner and Chile's Pinochet were practically precluded in Brazil. Such American "Brazilianists" as Thomas Skidmore (1973: 17–18) and Alfred Stepan (1973: 56–59) agree that, even while restricting decision-making authority to the most senior levels, consultation and adherence to the views of the majority far down the ranks was maintained, giving strength and some breadth of collective wisdom to choices the seniors faced about national policy and strategy.

Critics of the regimes in the early 1970s probably felt constrained to utter at least faint praise for the "miracle" economic records then being achieved; thus one finds laudatory statements within their prose, concerning the state apparatuses and their evident effectiveness, while noting the absence of compassion in the government's social policies. For example, Cardoso (1973: 158–59) roundly criticized the policies, but praised the efficacy and the conceptual foundations from which the regime undertook development and national integration programs. He noted that the system as structured, while increasing repressive capabilities, still had elements of dynamism in a more efficient state apparatus. Miguel Arrães (1972: 180–85, 190–92), while condemning the military for "imperialism," noted that the military elite once in power had built up middle-class support, introduced forms of technology, modernized the economy, and established new industries in the impoverished northeast region, which was still dear to him.

Whether or not one saw the internationalist policies that the ESG fostered as anti-nationalist seemed to depend upon whether the criticisms were based upon micropolitical choices and strategies or upon choices that warranted broad national approval. We see this in comments by Fernando Pedreira (1964: 14–18) regarding the way that old splits among the military elite over national petroleum policy—the 1950s Petrobras battle between nationalists and internationalists—tended to heal with early compromises worked out by leaders of the first and second government. (Amplification on this issue follows in subsequent discussions.) It was in the working out of specific aims and programs of those two governments, as well as in the three that followed, that the National Security Doctrine served a key role. In Dreifuss's (1981: 486) words, this was a "rudder" guiding the state. Yet, unaccountably, on the same page he seemed to conclude that that doctrine really had no goals, compared with those proferred by the Kubitschek administration, by which to inspire and arouse the Brazilian people.

POLITICAL INFLUENCE OF THE ESCOLA SUPERIOR DE GUERRA

We have commented on the larger numbers and higher ranks of senior officers on the permanent staff of the Escola Superior de Guerra, compared with larger graduate military institutions such as the U.S. National War College. There are other noteworthy indicators of the prestige within Brazil that has been attached to the ESG. For example, in each of the three pre–1964 presidential elections, one of the two major parties' candidates was an ESG graduate: Brigadier Eduardo Gomes (twice nominated), Marshal Juarez Távora, and Marshal Henrique Lott. (It might be noted that politics in Brazil, long before 1964, had been heavily penetrated by military influence.) Three of the five post–1964 military presidents—Castello Branco, Ernesto Geisel, and João Figueiredo—were either alumni or members of the ESG faculty. While President Figueiredo was serving the final two years of his six-year term, his younger brother (Gen. Euclides de Oliveira Figueiredo Filho) was the ESG commandant.

From such pieces of information, one can see that Brazilians might logically believe that the school held great political influence.

But what actual influence had the ESG exerted over the way military leaders conducted their governments? We are told that senior officials of the school steadfastly maintain that it did not enter into governing processes, limiting itself to development of the necessary knowledge to teach policy options and, by this means, to prepare military and civilian leaders for senior roles in the future execution of such policies (de Arruda 1983: xxiv). Two good measuring rods can be used to judge the political influence of the ESG: first, the extent to which ESG alumni later reached high policy-making positions; and second, the proportions of ESG military graduates elevated to the high command (general-admiral-brigadier ranks). By a longitudinal survey approach, each measurement should indicate whether graduates actually reached the echelon at which major policy decisions were being made. Additionally, we can examine the degree to which ESG doctrine found its way into active governmental usage through incorporation into law.

Senior Graduates in High Office

In the following surveys I attempted to preclude subjective judgments by establishing a rationale as to the criterion which should distinguish "high office" from positions of lesser import. Reliance was therefore placed upon authoritative directory sources and writings to identify occupants of positions engaged in highest policy discussions reported upon over the applicable years. This also will allow replication of my survey by anyone who has access to the typical sources of "Who's Who" in politics.

I divided the periods for analysis into three eras that I considered especially interesting: the late 1950s to early 1960s, the early 1970s (highest military dominance), and the early 1980s (when relinquishment of power was most earnestly debated). Lists of those who would be most influential in policy-making included the obvious choices such as the president, vice president, cabinet ministers, the president's civil and military advisers, prominent legislators (e.g., presidents of the Senate and Chamber of Deputies, and party leaders in Congress), and governors of the states most often considered as likely candidates for the next presidency (or, during the military rulership era when this was most unlikely, those most often cited by the major media and social science treatises). Each list was rounded off at thirty without difficulty, that number representing to me a reasonable number that might be truly prominent personages.

In checking the lists against the ESG Alumni Directory of Senior Course Graduates, I found the ratio of alumni occupying high positions did not vary much throughout the more than two decade interval. In the pre–1964 period, marked by high intrigue and anti-Goulart plottings, only six ESG alumni were found. These included Brigadier Gomes, former prime minister (and in 1985 "elected" president) Tancredo Neves, Marshal Odylio Denys (war minister), and three leading "plotters": Marshal Cordeiro de Farias (ex-governor of Pernambuco, but in 1964 *without* official duties[!]), General Castello Branco (at first Fourth Army commander, then Army chief of staff), and Gen. Pery Bevilacqua who was Second Army commander (São Paulo region). Each of these had a political following and claim to political power equalling that of the minister of war.

In the early 1970s period of the Medici government, the ESG alumni totaled eight, including presidential military adviser (and future president) General Figueiredo, Foreign Minister Mario Barbosa, Air Force Minister Marcio Souzo e Mello, Labor Minister Julio Barata, Transportation Minister (and future presidential candidate) Mario Andreazza, Mines and Energy Minister Dias Leite, and Senate President Virgilio Távora (son of Juarez Távora). To those, all then holding office, I decided to add Gen. Affonso Albuquerque Lima, the ex-minister of the interior who had been Medici's serious rival for the presidency, and who in opposition still held a measure of clout.

For the early 1980s, the ESG alumni again totaled eight. Those included President João Figueiredo, Mario Andreazza (now minister of the interior), and the three military ministers: José Magalhães Pinto (army), Bertholino Gonçalves (air force), and Henrique Saboia (navy). I also included three who were prominent opposition political figures: Tancredo Neves, governor of Minas Gerais and chosen as first civilian president; Severo Gomes, former trade and industry minister and, after his ouster, elected senator from São Paulo; and Gen. Euler Bentes Monteiro, ex-SUDENE president and later candidate against General Figueiredo in 1979, backed by the opposition party.

As can be seen from these lists, the attempt at quantified measurement of political influence reveals little change. Once we examine statuses of individuals, the impression grows that ESG influence actually may have declined.

Comparison of Military Alumni Promotions, 1950–1980

It should be noted that, while the ESG stood at the highest level of scholastic credentials, for the army officers the true hurdle for promotion to colonel and flag ranks was the Major Command and Staff School (ECEME), a three-year program with exceptionally competitive admission standards. Army Col. Eurico Sales Grande (1983: 160), not an ESG alumnus, candidly (and perhaps with some bias) described the school as

Table 2.1.
Promotion Rates by Services, 1950–1980

	1950	1955	1960	1965	1970	1975	1980*
Army	100%	100%	94%	55%	73%	56%	11%
Navy	100%	100%	64%	82%	72%	40%	22%
Air Force	100%	100%	86%	71%	90%	57%	44%
Overall	100%	100%	86%	67%	77%	52%	23%

* It should be noted that 1980 graduates were still within zones of promotion in this tabulation, and the indicated percentages would undoubtedly increase.

the "daughter of the ECEME," and stated that in his opinion the ESG did not amount to a "career-oriented course." This noted, it remains useful to see what pattern exists in the promotion rates to high command (i.e., general and equivalent) rank, by services, from 1950 through 1980.

There are two supplementary bits of information which need to be added in interpreting table 2.1 promotion rates. First, the service ministers and the EMFA General Staff ministry chose, in the period after 1964, to admit military members who were younger and less senior to the Senior Course. This meant there no longer would be the invariable expectation that such students were already promoted to general rank. Second, the "drawing power" of the school for senior officers in the post–1964 period perceptibly weakened because of the attractive alternative options presented, often competing with attendance inasmuch as the opportunity to attend was a crossroad not apt to be revisited. In conversations, few in number but seemingly representative, I found that officers in the eligible entry ranks were not, as a matter of career planning, expecting to attend, but would not like to decline if nominated.

As the data show, the ESG may have become a career "Siberia" in the 1960 to 1965 period, and it is no longer seen as an essential career credential. Some corroboration is given by the declining numbers of military enrollments, going from the high point of fifty-one in 1960 to present numbers averaging thirty-five in recent classes. Comparison of numbers of civilian attendees drawn from the "cooptive sector" (not sponsored by ministries or government agencies) is inconclusive, varying from twenty to twenty-five since 1960, with an unexplained valley of only fifteen in 1965.

Influence Claims By the School

In his concluding chapter, Arruda (1983: 295–99) summarizes the accomplishments and specific contributions toward enduring influence over Brazil's policy-making system. As a crowning achievement, he considers the ESG's "creation of a concept of global and integrated development," and the "diffusion within Brazil of new methods of team work at high levels, replacing individualism" to have been major contributions. He also cited these specific changes attributable to the ESG: placement of specific conceptual language regarding national security within the 1967 constitution; defining various aspects of national security which are found in Chapter 1 of the Law of National Security; the concept that every Brazilian bears responsibility for the national security, entered as Article 86 of the present constitution; and redefinition of the structure and responsibility of the National Security Council in Article 89, as modified on two subsequent occasions (Decree Law 200 of 1967, and Decree Law 900 of 1969). The latter item is probably the most notable, affecting the organ of government charged with establishing the nation's "permanent national objectives" and the foundations of subsequent national policy. In Brazil, the National Security Council consisted of the president, vice president, ministers of state (i.e., cabinet ministers), armed forces chiefs of staff, and the president's military adviser acting as the permanent CSN secretary general. Besides these basic laws, Arruda cited the basic principles now incorporated into law by which national planning and administrative reform are being prosecuted.

In documenting specific achievements of the ESG, Professor Arruda had the limited perspective of an insider. It seems probable that a clearer insight into the real influence of the school comes from observations of external evaluators such as Alfred Stepan (1973: 56–59), or Octavio Costa (1964: 69). Lieutenant Colonel Costa, who was not an ESG alumnus, perceived that the unity within the armed forces had been the result of long and careful preparation on the part of the ESG, emanating throughout the schools of command and staff, general staff, schools, bases, arsenals, barracks, and establishments. That degree of unity is the subject of subsequent investigation.

CONCLUSIONS

The initial composition and staffing of the Escola Superior de Guerra made it an unusual and highly significant institution of higher military education. Depending upon one's subjective viewpoint, it was either an illustrious or infamous center of political activism which Western traditions normally reject as unprofessional. I find it difficult, upon investigation, to fault its high principles and nationalist motivations, even if activism is to be regarded as a cardinal sin. Clearly, in spite of an unusual emphasis on civilian participation and staff contributions which is not often found elsewhere among "war colleges," it remained primarily a military institution. The ESG held undeniable policy influence, especially after the inauguration of the Castello Branco government, but also in later periods.

The alleged pro-American bias of the ESG was also evident in the first military government. However, political cooptation by U.S. advisers in league with Brazilian *entreguistas*—frequently asserted by observers cited above—has not been established, and would be denied vehemently by those in authority, then or now. It is not disputable, on the other hand, that the ESG and the Castellist policy line in government, because of their North American leanings, rather quickly lost support among rival elites. We saw this reflected in major changes of policy by the second military government. Subsequent events such as the waning of the Cold War, and the successful creation of an arms industry in Brazil, permitted greater independence in foreign policy and economic strategy, leading the ESG toward a more compatible, nationalistic perspective toward the external world.

The evidence examined in this study indicates that the political influence of the Escola Superior de Guerra is not now as great as it was during its first two decades. Compared with North American institutions, however, it still possesses far more policy influence than the U.S. National Defense University, or any comparable "war college." Considering only its educational role, it may have no more impact on decision processes, per se, than any other graduate educational institution. However, it still produces a more significant share of national leaders than one expects to find emerging from war colleges. Its role in leadership and influence throughout the Brazilian military services is still significant, and it has recognizable influence also within senior ranks of the civil service.

The Escola Superior de Guerra possesses an unusual luster, based upon mixtures of earned reputation and mythology, which makes it a durable national symbol. By this fact, it is reasonable to expect that the school can "live off its capital" for years to come. Surely it should have an important role for years to come in preparing new leaders to face challenging responsibilities in Brazil's drive toward its still-awaited destiny as a major world power.

3

Factors Tending to Divide the Armed Forces Internally

The high level of agreement that first chapter hypothesized to have existed among the military leaders in 1964 was based upon the conviction they were believed to hold that there were signs that the Goulart regime had lost its political base of support and was desperately reaching out to the revolutionary left, creating circumstances mandating the removal of that government. The second chapter examined the principles behind ESG-based studies concerning structural and political problems perceived to be major factors holding Brazil back from its destined emergence as a major world power. Out of those studies, the new leadership appeared determined to hold on to the reins of government, at least for a few years, with a "mission" of establishing the country on a new, progressive path—after the nation had been purged of populist and procommunist elements, and a new government had been launched upon a stable fiscal and economic policy.

Before considering how the new leadership faced its multiple governing challenges, there is an important preliminary question to investigate: with the first crisis behind them, what was the potential for fragmentation within the military elite over major ideologic issues? Fractures were quite possible in either of two areas: political ideology, or service-based generational self-interests. It is useful to begin such analysis with the period of Goulart's tenure as president, at a time when there was less risk of disunity due to the burden of direct responsibility for policymaking. Unity is an imperative, because preservation of order and resolution of political crises, by fiat if necessary, is a military responsibility. After 1964, the problem was apparent: a degree of disharmony might be tolerable, but top-level fracture must be averted at all costs. Drafters of the Law of National Security, which was embedded in the Constitution of 1967, realizing this, made it a serious crime even to publicly suggest that disunity existed within the armed forces.

One of the first corrective steps the new military rulers adopted was aimed at ending the widespread hostility which had been created under the Goulart administration over politicized processes of promotion and appointment of officers in senior ranks. The most obvious initial step was removal of those "political" leaders. New laws made advancement or forced retirement, once promoted to general, admiral or brigadier (air force senior rank), mandatory at every subsequent step. The total span of tenure in the upper four ranks was further limited to twelve years, with mandatory retirement in the four-star ranks at age 62. Within an environment that might have extended the politicization, and thus polarization, of the officer cadres, reform laws concerning the processes of assignment and advancement helped to instill a high degree of professionalism.

In addition to performance judgments recorded regularly by the responsible seniors, which is a practice common to most of the military professions, Brazil's officers bound for the upper ranks must pass through one or more post-graduate schools. For army officers, selection to ente its three-year, Major Command and Staff School (ECEME) is stiff enough to exclude three-fourths of those field grade candidates taking its entrance examination. The navy and air force have similar midcareer school requirements for the advancement to senior ranks. Officers of all three services may also be afforded the opportunity, selectively, to attend the ESG (Escola Superior de Guerra, nicknamed the "Sorbonne"), usually at the career point where they are apt to be promoted to general, admiral, or brigadier. Standards such as these clearly help to create a merit-oriented officer corps. Various external observers (Schneider 1971: 260, 291: Stepan 1973: 47; Manwaring 1978: 250) continue to identify Brazil as having the hemisphere's most highly professional military organization. Whether this might also tend to foster democratic attitudes is, naturally, debatable. An informed opinion about social behavior holds that one cannot be expected to undergo much change in personal values by midlife.

The proposition considered here is that divisions based upon personal ideologic beliefs, accentuated by different self-interests, will tend to emerge among generational or service-based factions. Issues of national importance might even threaten the ability to govern authoritatively, or result in upper-level fractures which could lead to fratricide. What issues? As Ernesto Geisel, the fourth military president, succinctly stated it (Loveman and Davies 1978: 193), all of Brazil's many problems could be placed in these two categories: development and security. But, as many others agree (Black 1980: 628–35; Manwaring 1978: 241; Druckman and Vaurio 1983: 303, 320), a third category—international relationships—should be included since Brazil so clearly needed trade and financial support abroad. Relations with the United States loomed large, but as we see today, Brazil's new horizons ranged far beyond the hemisphere.

Lacking the legitimacy that comes by way of free elections, Brazil's military leadership needed to present a united front in facing national issues, simply to carry out policies in such a way that public approval might create some de facto legitimacy. The unity requirement went beyond mere avoidance of threats of a coup d'etat or disruptive violence; it was necessary for major accomplishments. Morris Janowitz (1964: 67) has stated it best: "Cohesion—the feeling of group solidarity and the capacity for collective action—is an essential aspect of the military profession's internal organization that conditions its political behavior."

An early, almost assured asset toward earning public support would come from correcting the Goulart regime's serious errors. It would prove far more difficult, and more divisive within the new government and the military elite as a whole, to redirect and then move the nation toward renewal and growth on a broad front. With such changes contemplated, the military elite, now occupying some of the uppermost positions in government, could hardly be expected to remain isolated from influences of ideology and "politics." As a consequence, the armed forces soon found themselves almost totally immersed in the political pond. The press began to treat the semiannual publication of promotion lists as an exercise in "ticket balancing" among factions, despite the risk of violating the new Law of National Security. The common practice was to draw a distinction between those representing "moderate" and "hard-line" factions. Not all of those promoted bore such labels, and there were frequent misperceptions, but some of those who played the strongest roles displayed readily discernable policy leanings. The labeling practice had inevitable consequences in accentuating existing ideologic differences.

CONCEPTUAL BASIS FOR A STUDY OF THE MILITARY ELITE

In choosing not merely the repetitive chore of restoring the old political system of Brazil after destabilization, nor (as was initially asserted) the task of "saving Brazil" from sliding into a communist conspiracy, but rather, the long-range mission of launching the nation upon more progressive economic and political processes, the military leadership faced a lengthy and daunting period of likely internal divisiveness. My assumption therefore was that one of the first and most crucial aspects of analyzing the military rulership process and its results would be to undertake a methodical study of the degree of unity that was maintained throughout the 1964–1985 period. As a prefatory base, it would also be wise to examine unity prior to their entry into this unique stage of their collective experience as rulers.

Few North Americans, or for that matter Brazilians (so far as I am presently aware), have made serious efforts to investigate the political beliefs and ideologic attitudes of the military for logical reasons. Alfred Stepan (1971: 275) aptly described the subject of his seminal study as a "semi-closed institution" with little or no interest in self-disclosure. Others such as Schneider (1971), Manwaring (1978), and Black (1980) reached similar conclusions. With those forewarnings, I chose to study ideologic attitudes and unity by means of the essay literature published in the services' several periodical journals. Though not widely distributed outside Brazil, they are widely read within officer ranks. In prior publications (1985, 1986) I explained my focus upon development, internal security, and international relations as the issues most apt to be salient and divisive among military elites.

Research Design Aspects

This study of elite attitudinal differences attempts to discern and measure patterns of military concern and viewpoint regarding the three issue areas cited above: development policy, internal security, and international relations. An operational premise, based upon elite studies by various scholars, is that professional views expressed with the purpose of informing or influencing a peer group are relevant and measurable. Morris Janowitz (1960: 225), in his study of the U.S. military elite, stated: "Every profession assigns to itself a higher status than outsiders would be willing to concede, and every leadership group has a self-image which fails to correspond to the image that the public holds." Other scholars of military ideology (Feld 1964: 185–86; Stepan 1971: 84, 237; Stepan 1978b: 127–44), as well as others I have cited (Bacchus 1985: 101–02; Bacchus 1986: 403–5) elsewhere, have viewed the military elite's professional journals as a preferred representation of the "self image" of their profession. By a similar initial approach, Stepan (1978b: 127–44) researched the Peruvian military elite's ideology, using their journals.

The Self-Image. I define this concept as the self-regarding professional view which representative service intellectuals, such as journal editors and publishers, consider the existing or preferred professional attitude. Granting that the image may be consciously or subconsciously a bit elevated, as Janowitz has suggested above, it is no less relevant for our use here. As an exercise in influencing others, it passes from the theoretic to an operational level. It may be something published to burnish an author's reputation and promote career advancement—as has been one of the common side effects—but I share Maury Feld's (1964: 185–86) opinion that most authors have had as their primary motive the influencing of peers and seniors involved in the policy-making process.

Research Universe. The initial period of interest was the immediate period preceding the military takeover: 1963–1964. Subsequent analyses were selected at five-year intervals which would ordinarily match promotions and career reassignments. Great care had to be taken to select years that had not been overpoliticized by changes in the top leadership of each regime. Consequently, analyses of essay articles were made in the years 1963, 1968, 1973, 1978, and 1983. To avoid introducing personal biases through selective reading, every article authored by one or several Brazilian military officers (except for a very few of a narrowly confined nature devoted to such things as field tactics) in each of those years was read and analyzed. Using those rules, the study encompasses 417 articles published in Brazilian military journals over the five years indicated above. To the extent possible, effort was also made to obtain some balance in the numbers of periodical articles published by government bureaus and by the semiofficial club journals.

Methodology. In analyzing the self-image data, some of the familiar methods employed in content analysis were judged to be unsuitable for this study. Also, with research conducted under very limited resources in Brazil and the United States, it was not possible to pair my judgments with a second reader. The procedure adopted was to read each article completely, noting judgments as to the nature and level of the authors' attitudes in each of the three issue areas: development, security, and international relations. In each case, a preliminary step, which would permit anyone interested to replicate the study if they had the interest and resources, was to record complete imprints of each article, including biographic data on authors where it was available. For analytic purposes, the authors were categorized according to the three branches of the armed services, as well as by three rank/generational groups: senior officers (generals, admirals, and brigadiers), colonels and navy captains, and lower-ranked officers.

Even though it was anticipated that most essay articles might focus upon only one of the three issue areas, it was decided that each article would be judged on all three, since there could well be tendencies to overlap issues and patterns of change in attitude and emphasis that might otherwise be missed. It was also believed that this mode of analysis would not thereby overlook what might be institution-wide trends of interest on the part of authors or publishers.

For purposes of analysis, judgments were bracketed according to four levels of authors' interest: high, medium, low, or none. Those levels were scaled on a descending basis as 3—2—1—0, respectively, for the development and internal security issue areas. Guided by other observers' views (Schneider 1971: 354–55; Schneider 1976: 32–33, 74–75, 176–

77; Flynn 1979: 372–75, 488–89, 519; and Wesson 1982: 64–65), I treated nationalism and internationalism as opposites in judging external policy attitudes. To explain: ever since the "third option" era of Kubitschek's, Quadros's and Goulart's governments, nationalism has called for a greater departure from existing strong ties with the West, and (most of all) with the United States. Therefore, the extremes of the nationalism-internationalism axis were scaled at −2 for pro-socialist views, and +2 for views favoring the United States. Moderate nationalist (i.e., independence-prone) viewpoints, and those seen as pro-West (i.e., capitalist) were scaled as −1 and +1, respectively. One may question whether pro-socialist attitudes were correctly categorized, but the argument is moot: there was not one of the 417 articles classifiable as pro-socialist!

Finally, to provide aggregated data, the combined sums of ratings in each category were totaled and reduced to mean values, which were labeled as the "score" for that period. These aspects of the research design were established beforehand, and maintained throughout the research project. Conclusions were withheld in a few instances, because the number of essay articles authored in a category were less than the minimum number which would justify an assumption of normal distribution (Bacchus 1985: 102).

RESULTS OF THE ANALYSES

For each of the five periods selected, the reading-analysis-recording processes proceeded within a fairly compressed period. What are presented below are the results, preceded by information placing the issues confronting the military elite in historical context. Where this capsule view of events of the era failed to account for the deviances of authors in a category, an attempt was made to draw conclusions about what new perspective the data might infer or, alternatively, doubts which might arise as to how valid the deviances might actually be. Rather than attempting too quickly to reach judgments about the extent of internal disunity existing in a given period, conclusions were left to a final summation.

Growing Military Politicization in 1963

The start of 1963 seemingly promised a renewal of stability in government and strength in the economic outlook, based upon the five-to-one margin of the referendum restoring Brazil to its old form of presidential government, and the optimism generated from the Furtado Triennial Development Plan. The latter, however, had been based upon a restoration of credit internationally through major fiscal and financial concessions, to be achieved through negotiations with representatives of the World Bank and International Monetary Fund (IMF). Even though Brazil's annualized rate of economic growth exceeded that of its Latin American neighbors—about 6 percent on the average by the 1960s—debt repayments and importation costs for most of its technological and infrastructural needs were depriving its industrial sector of needed investment capital. The condition of the lower half of Brazil's society, meanwhile, was deteriorating under the demands of austerity which the IMF plan had demanded. In the Northeast, another serious drought had returned, impacting to some degree upon major center-south urban centers as refugees streamed in to depend upon state support.

After initially drawing up ambitious plans, Goulart's various ministers encountered strong resistance in Congress toward funding new labor and welfare legislation, drought relief works under the new SUDENE bureau, and other public construction programs. Funds were likewise not readily forthcoming from foreign lenders or the World Bank, because of the low opinion of Goulart and his administration following the 1961–1963 skirmishes, adding to widely held suspicions that he was an avid socialist if not a "closet communist." Those beliefs grew by mid–1963, when Goulart finally abandoned the austerity plan demanded by the IMF, as well as his triennial national development plan. With that turnabout and a series of political reversals, Goulart's stock in Brazil, and within the military leadership, steadily declined.

As we have seen in the preceding chapter, a much different atmosphere and style of policy deliberations was taking place in the ESG Senior Course, where outstanding officers of the three armed services and a slightly larger, comparably prestigious cadre of civilian professionals were assembled. Whereas Goulart and his cabinet ministers vacillated amid growing strains and the radicalizations initiated at the top, the ESG staff and students were ambitiously planning a new course for the country. In more private circles, a few staff members and former colleagues were also plotting either direct intervention or contingency plans in the event of a military intervention. As many were well aware, at least in the first half of 1963, there was by no means strong support for actual removal of the president; many of the so-called "legalist" faction within the military well remembered repercussions stemming from the previous interventions in 1954–1955, and believed that the wisest course was to remain aloof from "politics."

The essay samples anylized from the 1963 period totaled eighty-one, satisfactorily distributed among the three services, and the "seniors," colonels-captains, and the lower-ranked generational groups, to permit drawing statistically valid conclusions about ideologic differences. Having published a more detailed summation of the content and findings of the survey process elsewhere (Bacchus, 1985), it seems reasonable to limit presentation here to the salient differences which were revealed.

After finding the Chi Square test of significance somewhat less powerful than Kolmogorov's D Test—actually, the Chi Square test had seemingly exaggerated differences as well as degrees of consensus where they existed—I found that the literature published in military elite professional journals demonstrated a high degree of agreement on each of the three issue areas: development policy, internal security, and international relations. It is instructive, however, to look more closely at the few areas of discernible policy dissensus.

The area of greatest consensus in 1963 involved internal security policy, being a matter of some concern to the army, but of little importance to navy authors, and receiving much more attention from senior ranks than from either of the other rank groups. There was nearly equivalent consensus concerning development policy among the three service groups, and in fact the only statistically "deviant" rank group was that of the colonels and navy captains. Since only sixteen authored essays were available (just at the minimum number to be regardable as a sufficient sample), not too much significance should be attached to this item in the survey. Curiously, this group, which so often exhibits policy differences with the senior rank group whom they at times impatiently seek to replace, demonstrated less concern for national development! Their development policy score, midway between medium and low levels of interest and about 10 percent below the mean score for the eighty-one essayists as a whole, deviated statistically at the .05 level; that is, a result randomly anticipated to occur only five times out of a hundred examples. The question raised is whether these next generation military leaders were behaving as realists, out of a recognition that Brazil's immediate development prospects were unpromising for the near future, or whether they were perhaps unwilling to express deeper concern out of disagreement with the rhetoric of development which their seniors and national leadership more openly espoused.

The widest divergence of attitudes in 1963 was found in the international relations issue area, with navy authors very much alone in their display of internationalist and pro-Western views. All of the other services and each of the rank groups scored on the nationalist side, with the air force authors (significant at the one per one hundred level) most nationalist of all. This is possibly explained by their greatest dependence upon high degrees of technology, and by American and European nations' past reluctance to share such information with Latin American clients. It was not unexpected to see the navy express greatest interest in internationalism, in view of the lengthy history of American military assistance to Brazil's navy and Naval War College, and of the traditional concern of naval officers for interests abroad, based upon the need for naval support of maritime transport and military logistics. There had been U.S. naval advisors regularly attached to Brazil's naval schools since 1922, and an extensive involvement by Brazil's navy in the "Battle of the Atlantic" during World War II.

Differences of Attitude Emerge in 1968

The uncontested ratification by Congress of the military elite's choice for next president—Marshal Artur Costa e Silva, until resigning, the self-appointed minister of war (army)—and simultaneous enforcement of the authoritarian Constitution of 1967 seemed to promise a reasonably smooth period of progress for the military leadership and the nation. Because of the austere fiscal policies and improved income tax collection processes which had been introduced several years previously, by 1968 there was a surplus of government revenue and a very favorable rate of inflation in the nation. In fact, by imposing Antônio Delfim Neto's new "crawling peg" dollar-indexation policy, Brazil was poised for reentry and advancement toward international economic competitiveness by 1968—the first year of the so-called "miracle years," when its annual rate of economic growth exceeded 10 percent.

In almost every other possible way, however, beginning with wildcat strikes in the metallurgy industries of metropolitan São Paulo in April, Costa e Silva's regime had begun a downward spiral of public dissent and administrative repression by 1968. Whereas the second president had pledged to "humanize" (popularize) what was still being termed the "Revolution of 1964" in military circles, popular approval was being with held by students, priests, educators, underpaid civil servants (including much of the career cadre of the armed forces), and disgruntled politicians. The atmosphere seemed less than prerevolutionary, but still ripe for militants to undertake organized terrorism and minor guerrilla activities.

Most of the antiregime actions by guerrillas remained quite sporadic and uncoordinated prior to 1968. There had been a few terrorist bomb attacks in 1966, including one at the Recife airport which only missed President Costa e Silva (while "campaigning" in the unopposed October 1966 election) because of a mechanical delay. Then in 1967 a few bands of ex-army guerrillas, probably linked to exiled ex-Deputy Leonel Brizola's pre–1964 "Groups of Eleven" (Skidmore, 1988: 49, 86) which were to stand and fight if and when any military coup attempt threatened Goulart's presidency, struck at minor military posts in some of the less vital areas such as backlands Paraná and the interior of Minas Gerais and Espirito Santo. By 1968 Brazil's military faced not only repetitive bank "expropriations" styled after Uruguay's Tupamaros, but also committed guerrilla armies (to exaggerate somewhat their size) such as the ALN (National Liberator Action) organized by ex-deputy and longtime communist Carlos Marighela, and the VPR (Popular Revolutionary Vanguard) with ex-army Capt. Carlos Lamarca as leader during its most successful years. Many of those guerrillas, including Carlos Marighela, had obtained their guerrilla training in Cuba, though there was some training and assistance also given by other communist nations such as North Korea (Skidmore 1988: 87).

When faced with evidence of serious military opposition, it would be logical to anticipate that the military elite would be drawn closer together by the obvious need for unity in peril. As noted earlier, by 1968 there had been unmistakable division between hard-line and moderate groups of the military elite. For some, it may have been little more than personal factionalism between the two most senior leaders of the post–1964 movement: President Castello Branco and War Minister Costa e Silva, who clearly wanted to be president in 1964, and maintained his candidacy throughout the following three years by cultivating the authoritarian groups. Naturally, the internal security policy area furnished followers of the hard-line and Costa e Silva with something close to their hearts, about which they would differ vigorously with moderates inclined toward reforms in preference to police actions.

The Costa e Silva regime, whether willing to admit it or not, owed quite a bit to the first military government. Much of the potential wrath at austerity in the wages and benefits area, and at widespread purgings of suspected communists and corrupt politicians, had been spent by March 1967, setting the stage for more favorable public attitudes in years to come. While the rate of inflation was still abnormally high—ranging from 50 to 60 percent annually—there were signs of cooling of the consumer economy, even while investments from foreign sources had begun to reinvigorate the overall economy. And there was a cadre of highly qualified civil servants, recently engaged in the state planning and management processes, replacing some of the purged officials who owed their positions to patronage and leftist politics.

Along with the advantages he inherited, however, Costa e Silva had some carryover influences to contend with, especially within the upper ranks of the armed services, that were not to his liking. Due to the deep purges of senior ranks, who had owed their positions to President Goulart as "political appointees," the Castello Branco government had the opportunity to promote and position officers mostly drawn from the Sorbonnist line in all the key military and civilian posts which were customarily filled by members of each of the armed services. As president, Costa e Silva dared not now repoliticize the promotions and appointments process by cashiering those officers—usually men of exceptional competence—simply because of political differences. Moreover, under the guidelines of general, admiral, and brigadier forced retirements upon failing promotion at four-year intervals, it was likely that he would have those officers serving on active duty for as much as a decade to come. Obviously, their influence would outlast his own term as president.

One especially salient characteristic among each rank group in the 1968 period, important to each service but the navy, was concern over internal security. Because of rising levels of discontent among Brazilians of the lower and middle classes, in contrast to those of the upper echelon who enjoyed greater wealth, native and foreign volunteer revolutionaries judged the times to be ripe for mounting an insurrectionary challenge. Where some Brazilians may have seen the year as a beginning of "happy, stable days," as LaMond Tullis (1973: 89) observed, it soon became marred by bank robberies, kidnappings, and terrorist attacks on targets such as government and foreign consulate offices, or radio stations and television studios. When pressure mounted, and the urban police systems seemed incapable of apprehending the offenders, members of the authoritarian wing of the army agitated for an all-out assault to restore internal security. In data presented elsewhere (1985: 108), one finds the unity between services and even between rank groups by generations nearly sundered over the issue of whether to assume major responsibility for protecting internal security.

Other consequences of the new governing responsibilities assumed since 1964 seemed to emerge from the survey of the eighty-eight military-authored essays in the 1968 period. On each of the three issue areas, distinct differences of attitude and levels of perceptible concern showed up between army and navy essayists. It would have been nice to see where the air force authors stood, since they too might well have viewed ruling responsibilities in a very different manner; unfortunately, in this and each subsequent year, there were too few essays by officers of the air force to permit statistically sound conclusions to be drawn. Among each of the three generational rank groups (within which essayists of the air force could be included), some significant differences once again emerged. Authors in the senior ranks (i.e., generals, admirals, and brigadiers of the air force) held the strongest views about being active in the internal security role, and—surprising to me—they also had the least nationalist, most pro-Western attitude of all in the international relations issue area. Those nearest to them in seniority (i.e., colonels and navy captains) seemed to differ most strikingly in both international relations and development policy aspects. The evidence seems to bear out the suggestion cited earlier, that there was a strong "Castellista" influence imparted to Brazil's senior military ranks in the wake of the purging of many Goulart-appointed leaders, whose places were then filled by early promotions of intellectually minded, pro-American "Sorbonnists." Along with navy authors as a group, it was the colonels-captains group who scored highest (both above 2.0 scale), indicating medium to high interest in development policy, and highest by far in the nationalist direction on international relations attitudes. As an eventual successor group to their seniors, it appears that colonels consciously detached themselves from what may have appeared to be an excessively Western-dependent stance taken since 1964.

By 1968, the government was fully launched upon Delfim Neto's strategy for becoming a globally competitive producer of a variety of commodities and manufactured goods. A corner piece of that plan involved the curbing of demand-side inflationary pressures through rigid control over working-class wages. This in turn called for government control over unions and merchants, which tended to draw the ire of the legislature and the progressives of the Catholic clergy. News media and students soon added to the pressures that were to fall upon Costa e Silva, possibly leading to the stroke in late August 1969 that disabled the second military president, and by year's end led to his death. In the meantime, the high command of the armed forces, acting much like a "College of Cardinals," selected General Emilio Garrastazú Médici to be his replacement. Despite the setback of once-announced intentions to "humanize" and eventually redemocratize Brazil's governing system, economic recovery was already underway, leading toward the so-called "miracle years." At the same time, and perhaps for that very reason, the military elite was unwilling to step aside and let Vice President Aleixo be installed as an interim, civilian president. It was with that environment, beset for a few years with urban guerrillism, that the five-year term of the Médici government began.

Repressions Amidst Economic Boom in 1973

In many ways, the final year of President Médici's extended term found the military elite under new pressures, even as it held out promise for awhile as the start of Brazil's rise as a major world power, with flourishing trade moving now into promising new market areas such as Japan, China, and the Soviet Union. Though Brazil was importing more than three-fourths of its consumption of crude oil, the economic impact of rapid OPEC price escalations had yet to make its full impact upon a very favorable balance of foreign trade accounts. Much of the pressure on the leadership stemmed from the delicacy with which commitments and promises of political benefits had to be allocated between hard and moderate factions of the armed forces, as selection of a successor began. Federal revenues, meanwhile, were by 1973 rising so handsomely as a result of much-improved tax collection techniques that the Médici government saw the opportunity to undertake ambitious infrastructure projects, and simultaneously to fund social welfare and regional development projects of major proportions in the South, Northeast, and Amazon basin states. It was a very good year in many ways.

The threat of guerrilla attacks was much reduced by 1973, the Cold War abroad was perceptibly abating, U.S. withdrawal from Vietnam was nearing its end, and the spirit of détente was growing stronger in the aftermath of the major powers' summits in Beijing and Moscow. It is generally agreed now that the antiregime guerrillas had been virtually defeated by mid–1971. However, throughout 1973, much of the military right wing and some of the revolutionary left were refusing to concede their defeat (Fiechter 1975: 147; "Pau de Arara" 1972: 108–21). Whereas the mean score on the internal security issue, from data based on eighty-two military essayists published elsewhere (1985), was now only 1.35 (i.e., closer to the "low" level of intensity than to "medium" level), among senior ranks the scoring ran above the midpoint between the two levels. For colonels and captains, on the other hand, recognition of the declining threat was apparent; their score was only slightly above 1.0 (i.e., "low" concern). It seems probable that the sustained level of concern among seniors was prompted more by the "politics" of prolonging military roles in internal security than by anxiety over further guerrilla threats.

Differences of attitude continued to show up in the essays published in 1973 between army and navy authors, and even more so between the colonels-captains and their seniors, on each of the other two issue areas as well. Once again, the highest degree of interest in development policies was perceived among navy authors, and significantly less for the first time by army essayists. On the international relations issue area, however, now it was navy authors who showed much greater nationalism than those of the army, though by now the pattern of national rather than international attitudinal views become universal. Factors such as "détente," the ending of the Indochina conflict, and rapid globalizing of trade may have exerted some influence. A reading of the professional journal literature suggests, however, that the number one topic on the authors' minds was national development policy. There was a sense of new urgency about making the best possible use of resources that might erode or slip away, if not correctly and diligently applied.

The nationalism theme increasingly was becoming more evident in the articles authored by the senior ranks, where such sentiments were nearly a universal point of view. Among the colonels' group, the nationalism score was even less than for authors in the lower ranks. There is a certain rationality in these kinds of differences, which incidentally measure statistically significant at the .01 level (i.e., apt to occur randomly once in a hundred cases). In the 1968 literature survey, the lower-ranked group was all alone with an "internationalist" (i.e., bias toward pro-Western views and interests) score of + .11, and the colonels' group stood out as the most nationalist with a score of − .31, again of significance apt to recur randomly once in a hundred or more cases. One only needs to grasp the generational trend, whereby those who were colonels and naval captains in 1968 would likely be generals and admirals (or else retired) in 1973. Similarly, some of those below colonel rank might now be in the colonel author group.

Moderating Trends and Economic Anxiety in 1978

Whereas the final year of President Médici's government was marked by optimism over the rising economic health of the country, President Geisel in his final year was far less fortunate. Even so, the economic unsettlements afflicting the nation could not unite the armed forces leadership in the same way their seniors had faced the political crisis of 1963–1964. As subsequently indicated through the survey of professional literature of the 1978 period, it seems clear that viewpoints of those actively engaged in debating policy issues became less impassioned, perhaps accountable to their appreciation of the small role the military leadership was equipped to play in this new arena of macroeconomic policy.

The one most frequently mentioned economic policymaker of the 1970s in Brazil was the Costa e Silva and Médici minister of finance, Antônio Delfim Neto. Though probably best known internationally for initiating the continuous monetary adjustment process which he labelled the "crawling peg" (i.e., cruzeiro to dollar indexation at intervals as frequent as monthly), Delfim's involvement in the industrial and, later, agricultural expansion actually made him a major factor in Brazil's energetic drive to become a competitor in world commodity and even manufactures exports. Monetary value corrections became indispensable to that effort, due to the accepted inevitability that the inflationary pressures and global disadvantages Brazil faced were devaluing the cruzeiro at a faster rate than most European and Japanese monetary values. The correction process was also a major factor in the attracting of foreign investors, who were by the mid–1970s becoming especially drawn toward Brazil as a hot prospect for investing the influx of "petrodollars" which were being deposited annually.

When President Geisel, who had come to the office from the post of president of Brazil's largest state enterprise, PETROBRAS, assumed the presidency in 1974, the impact of the OPEC price hikes for crude oil—which Brazil needed for more than three-quarters of its fuel consumption—had not yet been fully felt. However, Geisel made it obvious from the start that he intended to exert a personal influence over fiscal policy. Whereas Delfim Neto wanted the nomination as next governor of São Paulo state, he was rewarded by being shunted off to Paris as the Brazilian ambassador to France. With Delfim out of touch, Geisel's somewhat different policy views and considerable experience in matters of international trade and finance stood a much better chance of being accepted among the industrial elite of the country, most of whom were *Paulistas*.

Though foreign trade was growing rapidly by 1974, the ability of the nation to continue that growth and favorable balance was becoming doubtful. Inflationary pressures were causing the cruzeiro to devalue internationally, and because of greater energy costs, the rate and costs of production were responding adversely to price trends at the same time that Brazil faced rising rates of interest and debt service payments. At the same time, similar inflationary effects abroad were raising the costs of imported capital equipment and technology. In this economic squeeze, it became apparent that the crawling peg system of monetary adjustments at short intervals deserved to be renamed the "trotting peg." Internally, policy makers sought somehow to retain hard-won market entry gains by holding down labor costs through underreporting of cost of living index data. Inevitably, this aggravated the government's relations with civil servants and labor union interest groups. Times were tough.

One consequence of the dollar indexation system was to arouse latent anti-Americanism—feelings already sensitized by evidence of Brazil's continuing dependency upon the economic base in the United States, which remained its largest single market even while trade had been expanded to new areas. When the dollar began its own accelerated depreciation of value in relation to other major world currencies by the late 1970s, along with rapidly increased interest rates on the "rolled-over" loans Brazil had entered into several years earlier, the tendency was to cry "foul!" It seemed quite natural to Brazilians to see themselves as victims of what appeared to be mismanagement and petroleum/energy profligacy. In this matter, as in many others, the armed forces were as closely attuned and sympathetic to public sentiments as were civilians.

The literature survey of 1978 reflected the growing sense of nationalistic awareness and of separation from the former, pro-Western and pro-American attitudes their predecessor authors had held. Even though the overall score was somewhat less (−.29 in 1978, compared to −.39 in 1973), there was far less difference between the army and navy authors, and between senior officers and the colonels-captains group in 1978 than formerly. Generational consistency was again evident, especially so for former "lower ranks" who were presumably now colonels and navy captains, with virtually identical scores over each period. Former colonels who would be among the generals-admirals-brigadiers group in 1978 were much less nationalistic than their 1973 predecessors, but more so than the colonels-captains group of that year. Events cited above seem an adequate explanation of the trend toward nationalism.

It happens, however, that there were other, more specific incidents which unquestionably accentuated the trend within the nation at large toward perceptible anti-Americanism in the 1978 period.

Though President Geisel's announced intention to liberalize political processes with his *distensão* (decompression, or less literally, relaxation) policy must have been noted with satisfaction in State Department circles in Washington, the Carter administration seemingly turned on Brazil's leadership by publicly including the country among its targeted governments accused of serious violations of human rights. Coming somewhat after the era of worst abuses, and running counter to the Brazilian government's now pressing need and desire for sympathetic treatment abroad when it was beset with financial woes, the reaction in Brasilia was one of disappointment and anger. To that same end, the pressures placed upon Brazil to commit itself to signature of the nuclear nonproliferation and nuclear-free zone measures (Tlátelolco Agreements) were yet another annoyance. The ultimate breaking point came when the United States attempted, in retaliation for Brazil's noncompliance, to cut off delivery from West Germany of the fissionable nuclear reactor material which was essential to the operation of the second and subsequent nuclear power plants—Angra dos Reis II, III, etc.—after having curtailed the contracted technological and fissionable materials deliveries by the Westinghouse Corporation, which had cooperated on Brazil's first nuclear power plant, Angra dos Reis I.

The disaffection between the two nations thereafter intensified. Brazil determined at about that point to become a major munitions and military technology producer on its own, managing within the next decade to export so much military matériel that it became the world's sixth largest military arms exporter, not far behind China, France, and the United Kingdom. No longer finding itself in need of American military advisers, it also closed the U.S. Military Assistance Mission, which had by then become more ornamental than helpful.

In the other two attitude components, particularly internal security concerns, there had been very little change since 1973. Whereas the score on development attitudes rose to 1.87 (almost averaging "medium" levels of interest, and equalling what was seen in 1963), the internal security score dropped further, to 1.18—little above a "low" level of concern. There was not much sign of active insurgency except in the Amazonian state of Pará, where a minor Marxist foco established near Araguaia had survived all past paramilitary sweeps. It was now becoming a concerted rights-abuse focus of the Catholic activists who were building up communities of lay persons to challenge the government's policies of mineral production as part of the *Grande Carajás* project, and the continuing program of *Nordestino* peasant relocation as part of the Program of National Integration (PIN) and TransAmazon Highway development program. Even though widely reported as extinguished, Araguaia remained, almost alone, an outpost of guerrilla defiance (Lernoux 1982: 267–77).

Difficulties with the Democratic Transition in 1983

The specific discussion of Brazil's transition to civilian leadership, and of hard-line resistance to President Figueiredo's *Abertura* project in particular, is reserved to a following chapter. At this point, the object is to indicate how differences of views toward power-wielding policy were reflected—if only slightly, as will subsequently become evident—in the essay literature of the military professional journals. Actually, the survey results do suggest that greater harmony existed within the armed forces elite than published opinions by the journalists at the time reflected. This contradictory finding is not necessarily to be discredited; rather, it may be explained by the perception of those times that the appearance of discord within the military was only a consequence of the greater freedoms of expression which both elements—press and armed forces members—were now enjoying.

Prior to leaving office, President Geisel canceled the broad emergency powers of the presidency which Costa e Silva had decreed by Institutional Act #5 in 1968. Upon assuming office in March 1979, President Figueredo accelerated the political "opening" process by abolishing the recognizably farcical, two-party system, and by pushing through the Congress a general amnesty law which encouraged exiled radicals such as Leonel Brizola, Miguel Arrães, and Luis Carlos Prestes to return. Congress stopped short, however, of legalizing the Communist Party, of which Prestes was still leader. The lack of legal status had never inhibited the PCB from publishing its views on issues, nor of maintaining headquarters in major cities. Thus, in the 1982 elections, for the first time in more than seventeen years open to selection of every office except the presidency, the PCB even published endorsements of candidates in one or another of the opposition parties.

Official proclamations commemorating the occasion of the November 1935 communist insurrections in Rio de Janeiro and in the Northeast always represented a time when the most vigorous expressions against the "communist threat" by military spokesmen appeared in the press. When combined with the specific alarm diehards felt over such events as the election of Leonel Brizola as the next governor of Rio de Janeiro state, it was not hard to keep the anticommunist sentiments alive. However by 1983 such viewpoints represented only a minor element of the military elite, according to the survey of essay literature. While scores on the internal security issue area were reaching an all-time low, there was now a near consensus of attitudes moving toward nationalism, and away from pro-Western internationalism, as the detailed data published elsewhere (1985:115) clearly indicated.

Circumstances known to have affected Brazil's military elite ideologically accord well with my 1983 survey of the literature. Animosity toward the United States probably peaked at the time of earlier incidents during the Carter administration, but that feeling did not soon recede. The Reagan administration alienated more Latin Americans than it appeased by decisions taken in 1982 and 1983 over conflicts in the South Atlantic (Malvinas) and Grenada. Greater discord ensued after the American government adopted its interventionist measures in Central America. In what may seem to be a perverse twist, even the Pentagon's decision to invite Argentinian military advisers to assist our military advisers in El Salvador in opposing the (alleged) subversive aims of Nicaraguan FSLN (*Sandinista*) "volunteers" surprised and annoyed some of the Brazilian army supporters of the moderate international line. After all, they reasoned, hadn't Brazil a far better record in terms of both antiguerrilla actions and the avoidance of extreme uses of state terrorism to uncover enemies of the state? In the 1983 survey, army scores on the international issue area bear out the growing nationalistic attitude.

The general reduction of expressed interest in development policy is another significant observation derived from the 1983 literature survey. It seems clear that Brazil's debt repayment problem and its inevitable impact upon development programs was a matter of grave concern. Therefore it must be deduced that by 1983 relatively few "experts" cared to test their career reputations in print by offering policy-oriented suggestions on ways Brazil could resume its economic growth path. Perhaps it now seemed best to let the civilians figure things out. From his interviews at the time with senior military leaders, Stepan (1988:115) concluded that many felt it was time to step aside, if only to better preserve their institutional interests at a time when each service had been enduring declining fiscal resources, as a by product of the nation's economic distress.

SUMMARY AND CONCLUSIONS

Inherent limitations in my employment of subjective evaluation of the elite attitudes on major issue areas have been reduced and nearly eliminated, since the focus has been shifted away from the judgments per se, to note changes of aggregated "scores" and to attempt conclusions based upon evidence of significant deviations from mean scores for each period chosen for investigation. Other scholars such as Max Manwaring and Jan Knippers Black, in their attempted analyses of military elite ideology—admittedly a very sensitive and therefore difficult proposition—found it necessary to employ methods no less subjective, and also confined to much briefer periods. Manwaring (1978:248), using a content analysis of major speeches of presidents and senior cabinet officials, found that more than 60 percent of speech content had focused upon the definition of development goals, and that aspects of national prestige and of internal security policy ranked second and third in emphasis. Black (1980:633), by means of a few interviews and additional informal conversations with senior military officials, noted a pronounced trend early in the Figueiredo administration, of what she termed *de rigueur* anti-Americanism. It seemed to her that Brazilian military leaders had moved sharply away from what had formerly been fondly termed an "unwritten alliance" with the United States. Each of those perceptions has been borne out in this study, using the published professional literature. At this point, it becomes necessary to assess the overall pattern and to detect trends in the military elite attitude.

The Pattern of Attitudes, 1963–1983

To better appreciate differences over time as well as between generational and service groups, a graphic presentation such as Figure 3.1 below becomes essential. In that figure, the mean scores on each of the three issue areas is represented by the dashed line, while symbols have been used to differentiate individual scores for each of the five intervals. To alleviate clutter while showing all three graphs in juxtaposition, the scores for the air force (because of underrepresentation for most periods) and of the lower-ranks group were eliminated, but were included in mean scores.

Upon viewing the graphs together, a first impression will be that the international relations area constituted the most divisive issue area. That impression is not entirely inaccurate; however, in the interest of better presentation, the vertical scale for that graph was expanded by 50 percent. Even so, the one clear trend which emerges is in that issue area. Nationalism unmistakably grew, period by period, as the military regime acquired maturity. Only navy authors exhibited notably internationalist attitudes, collectively, in the first decade of the analyzed period. Their view, consistent with the more external nature of their mission as well as their close association over an interval of five decades with senior instructors of the U.S. Naval Mission to Brazil, should have been anticipated. Yet, after that initial decade of military rulership, they too began to turn toward nationalism by the early 1970s, as the graph shows.

Another recognizable trend appears in the internal security issue area. So-called "professional" military services do not ordinarily dwell extensively on internal affairs including matters of security, which they view as "police work," preferring to be regarded as their nation's guardians against any external menace. Thus, when the security implications of

Figure 3.1. Attitude Scores on Issue Areas, 1963–1983

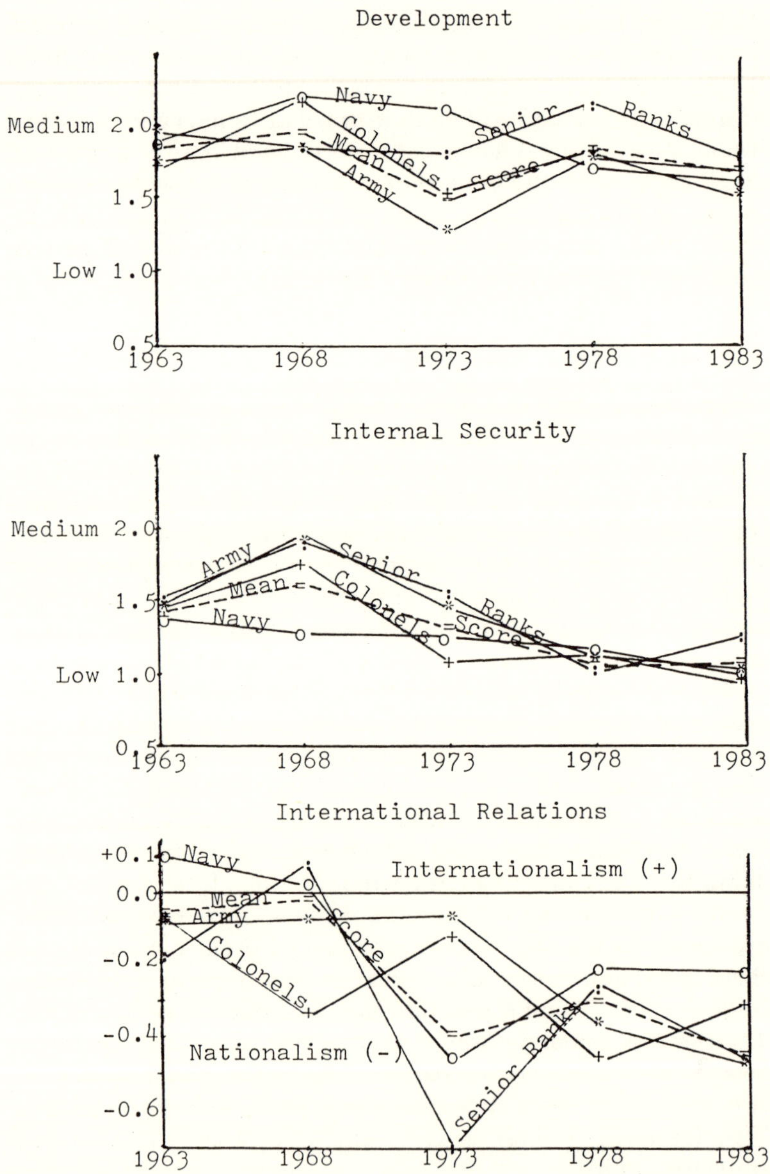

the Cuban Revolution and subversive infiltration by purveyors of international communism suddenly grasped the attention of members of the military elite, there was an immediate rush of authorship intent upon exploring (and often, exhorting) a new role for their services. Brazil's period of concentrated concern over internal security was equally quick to wane, following the successful and not very lengthy campaign of the late 1960s to early 1970s. As could be expected, thereafter there were relatively few essays that dwelt upon the internal security menace, and in cases of essays with a more general perspective on Brazil's (or their own service's) security preparedness, counter-guerrilla operations held only minor attention and concern. As professionals, authors were once again more apt to think and write about potential needs of the country and their respective services to deter or, if it should ever become necessary, defend the national territory and interests against a potential aggressor.

Something of a sinusoidal pattern appears, at least where the overall means scores are represented, on the development issue area. Little can be drawn from that pattern, except to remark upon the old and apparently ever-continuing pattern, for Brazil especially, of economic boom-bust-boom-bust variations. Inevitably, those are influential in the outlook and attitudes taken by military leaders who have ideas and proposals to offer toward the betterment of the country and their services. Of course, the cycles of economic advances and recessions have longer wavelengths than five to ten years. Still, the small undulations detectable in the graph of development attitude scores seem to reflect the two periods of the late 1960s and late 1970s when Brazil was poised to ascend to its long-awaited "takeoff" into developed, major power status. It may seem curious that the 1973 score in this area showed a drop. It may have been an aberration, but it could also have been the result of what may be called transition politics. Within the present and following years, power was due to shift to the Geisel administration—yet to be designated by the military high command—with its attendant uncertainties. There is no question that the advent of regime transitions affected career concerns and daily ministrations of those officers most apt to author essay articles, and there may also have been a tendency toward greater caution and repressed impulses to propose new initiatives among such men.

Finally, there may be some doubt about the validity of the survey results in the area of international relations, because of rather wide variations between the two services (army and navy), and between the senior-ranks group and the colonels-captains group, once again in the 1973 period. A review of the way the survey findings correlated with differences of self interests and group perspectives, however, tends to support as valid those periods of wide variance in international affairs attitudes.

CONCLUSIONS

In summarizations above, it was concluded that whatever subjectivity may have existed in my judgment process, in scoring the several hundred essays, that source of bias should have been eliminated by basing assessments on trends and results of the changes over time and between subgroups of the authors. It does not, however, rule out the possible presence of subjective bias among the publishers and editors in their choices of what to publish. The fact that there was not one essay over the twenty-year period which I categorized as "pro-socialist" in viewpoint does suggest the possibility of a bias, or of an imposed censorship. That "censorship," however, would in all probability not require any official directive; rather, it would normally tend to come about through the natural reticence of those favoring socialism to expose themselves to subsequent discrimination by seniors in a regime firmly committed to Western-style economics and global politics. Though this survey of professional literature may well be an imperfect vehicle for studying attitudes within the military elite, it appears to be more objective than alternative methods such as in-depth interviews with leaders who would not have obtained high statuses without having learned very well not to reveal, for attribution, viewpoints apt to arouse any adverse reactions among colleagues and political superiors. In the same way, speeches are invariably so well reviewed in advance of delivery to be unexceptional if not utterly bland, at least in terms of revealing unique or even uncommon viewpoints about major issues.

My judgment of the overall results of the survey of group and service differences of ideology is that there is nothing of a very strong or serious nature separating service branches or rank groups. Certainly this study has not revealed likelihood of a breach within the military elite, over any period, comparable to what has been commented upon on several occasions in the North American press. Of course, coming at this time, the accusation that I have exercised perfect hindsight could fairly apply. In fact, however, judgments of the content of essays had been made (and never subsequently in any way altered) within a year or two after each of the five time periods. They were not all reviewed in the 1984–1985 period, as some critics might suppose.

This investigation needs to take another step, however. With strong evidence that there were at least two important ideologic factions—so-called "hard-liners" and "moderates"—tending to taken turns in the leadership over the twenty-year period, another look should be taken at such philosophical groupings, to see if there was a potential for injurious cleavage within the elite. Was there a division which did not aggregate as an interservice or intergenerational faction, but collected instead along recognizable ideologic divisions? That investigation is the subject of the next chapter.

4

Ideology and Politics: A Second Look at the Unity Problem

In the preceding chapter, we obeyed a natural impulse in looking for signs of rivalry and division within the armed forces along lines of service and rank group self-interests. As Theodore Wyckoff (1965: 266) put it: "The political orientation of military personnel varies with the grade, age, and experience of the individual concerned," with "experience" normally subsuming one's service orientation. Yet, in our survey of Brazilian military elites, we found divisions along service and rank group lines to be no more than one expects to find, and perhaps less, considering the stresses placed on the services to obey seniors and uphold unity while involved in nonmilitary, essentially policy-related activities. But that survey also revealed what appeared to be a continuity of ideologic division along the investigated issue areas of development policy, internal security concerns, and views on international relations. It seems important, therefore, to further investigate what might be lying behind those persistent labels, "hard-line" and moderate, in discussions by the media of inter-elite divisions.

Some differences of view derived from the belief by a large group of so-called "professional" or "barracks" officers (Barros, 1985: 64) that military professionals' only appropriate role should be that of defending the nation against external foes, leaving to the politicians the control over constabulary forces, and the task of preventing internal revolts or subversions. That viewpoint gained adherents following the successful suppression and defeat of urban guerrillas, when their apprehensions over Castroism substantially diminished. On an opposite side, the hard-liners (also identified as "authoritarians") felt that it had only been through hard-own victories and continued vigilance that restoration of peace and civil order permitted their misguided colleagues to feel secure now. But their concern for preserving the civil order had a self-interested aspect, since military involvement in internal security conveyed enhanced powers and perquisites to the army, and to a lesser degree also to the air force. In fact, military police dominated the urban scene throughout the decade of the 1970s.

Those members of the military elite who believed that Brazil's fortunes rested in a continuation of its past close alignment with the West—particularly, with the United States—parted ideologic company with their peers who subscribed to the post–1950s "third option" proposition that neither East nor West should be treated as an ally. Since the natural term for the latter group was "nationalists," it seemed only fitting for external observers and the press to label as "internationalists" those hewing to the policy of the first military president, Castello Branco, who steered Brazil back into the orbit of the United States and the West. Later on, pragmatists of an "internationalist" persuasion may have joined nationalists in condemning excesses of Castellism as having sold out the nation's interests to Western capitalists. If true, those viewpoints did not emerge from my survey of the professional military literature, even in the latter periods.

Though the practice of openly espousing ideologic views has been untypical within the military elites in Ibero-American history, the recent behavior of leaders in the Brazilian armed forces may portend a different future norm, at least among the senior ranks. Thus, Wyckoff (1965: 272), whose first-hand observation of Latin American military elites was based upon earlier years as a member of the U.S. Military Mission to Brazil, seemingly regarded the remarkable political activism of junior army officers (revered in the 1930s as the "tenentes") to have been an aberration. He expected their activism to vanish as the officers reached midcareer.

The evidence of 1950s–1960s senior activism contradicts that expectation. Marshal Juarez Távora and General Henrique Lott of the army, and Brigadier Eduardo Gomes unsuccessfully campaigned for the presidency—Gomes did so twice. Marshal Eurico Dutra was elected president after the army ousted Getúlio Vargas. Távora served President Castello Branco as minister of transportation, and Marshal Cordeiro Farias—another ex-tenente, and past governor of Pernambuco state—served as minister of interior. On the other side, ideologically, Luis Carlos Prestes—ex-tenente who led the famous Prestes Column in campaigning to overturn the political system—headed the Brazilian Communist Party from the 1930s to the 1980s. The tradition of activism has long-standing precedents in Brazil.

FACTIONALISM ON NATIONAL DEVELOPMENT POLICY

Within the first year after military ruler began, two diametrically opposed camps developed among the elite. As so often happens in countries at Brazil's stage of political development, each camp thereafter was identified as if it had been based upon a purely personalist foundation. The *Castellista* group were neither clearly democratic nor authoritarian in outlook, and thus by definition became known as moderates n regard to their approach toward aggregating ruling power. The first military government mobilized elite support within the nonmilitary sector in a manipulative manner, but resisted friendly outsiders' entreaties to seek stronger public support, or to more fully normalize democratic processes. Seemingly, they wanted the trappings of a democratic system—as when Castello Branco insisted, against others' advice, on holding elections on schedule in 1965—but witheld the meaningful diffusion of political power. The *Costista* faction, so named for the second general-president, was fond of generating public demonstrations of approval, yet it practiced highly authoritarian means to gain and maintain ruling power, unhampered by any dependence upon the public will, or even symbolic support when the regime had fallen into disarray.

From the outset in the first regime, it was clear that the Castello Branco government was eager to welcome American business investments on an equal, or sometimes preferential, footing vis-a-vis Brazilian enterprises, in areas of taxation and regulation. This was one of the prime areas of disagreement on the part of the Costista faction, and it became also the view of the majority of Brazilians who did not stand to gain personally from any new opportunities thus created. By the time Costa e Silva began "campaigning," unopposed, for the presidency in each state, he became as much a nationalist as an authoritarian, at every stop promising he would "popularize" his government. He evidently intended to make some sharp shifts in development plans and foreign policy; but once he was elected little change resulted.

There were other factions within the Brazilian armed forces, as will be further discussed shortly. But first, let us deal with the intriguing question the above ideologic differences pose: why didn't this enmity, deeper than personalism, paralyze the elite? The unity of the armed forces leadership in 1964 had been based upon urgent considerations of security and national economic ills. By the late 1960s, with a rapidly improving economy, those unifying factors were no longer available. My answer, considered on the basis of circumstances and specific events such as the "coup within the Coup" in October 1965, is that there had to have been some sort of fail-safe compromise agreement, which I am labeling the "alternation agreement." In all probability, some type of compromise agreement was worked out in an "everybody wins" manner, at a moment when hard-liner hotheads led by General Albuquerque Lima, who was to become Costa e Silva's minister of the interior, wanted to remove Castello Branco forthwith, being outraged by the loss of key governorships in Rio de Janeiro and Minas Gerais states to the opposition. That loss was being taken as a personal affront—one that a military president should have been cautious enough to have prevented, or at least to have annulled.

The "Alternation Agreement"

Before presenting my hypothesis about what I believe was agreed upon in 1965, some factual information will help to clarify that which follows. We know that Costa e Silva, as War Minister (later to be titled Army Minister), went to Rio de Janeiro's suburban Vila Militar (military compound) shortly after the president had made clear his resolve to guarantee assumption of office by the two opposition governors. By then there were unmistakable signs that the garrison was preparing to stage a coup d'etat, probably by the next morning. After lengthy discussions, troops placed on alert were ordered to stand down, and Costa e Silva that same evening went to see Castello Branco for urgent negotiations. In the immediate aftermath of those talks, the very complexion of the Castello Branco administration changed dramatically. Changes began with the issuance of the Second Institutional Act and subsequent Complementary Acts by which the multiparty system was abolished in favor of the artificial, two-party experiment, and direct elections of future governorships (and of major cities and state capitals) were no longer allowed. In effect, only the election of legislators and municipal councils would be open to popular electoral processes.

This was the agreement which I believe was worked out following the October 1965 elections fiasco: (1) there was to be no coup, then or ever; (2) Costa e Silva was to have no opposition, civilian or military, in his bid to become the next president; (3) subsequent presidencies were to be alternated between the moderate and hard-line factions, continuing for as long as the High Command deemed it necessary that it retain direct control over the political system; and, (4) each president was to name as his army minister the senior active duty general of the opposite faction from that which he represented, as a reliable guarantor of the president's conforming with this agreement. There may have been also a clause specifying that the nomination—tantamount to "election" by the Congress—of subsequent presidents was to be decided by the convening and collective choice of the High Command. Since an enlarged "nominating council" was summoned in the case of the midterm replacement of Costa e Silva following his stroke and (ultimately) fatal illness, there is no convincing evidence that there had been a specific agreement about that aspect. The term "High Command" also is ambiguous, often being used for the dozen generals of four-star rank in the army. In the context of this hypothesized agreement, as evident from actual practice in presidential nominations, the "High Command" would have included another ten or eleven navy and air force admirals and brigadiers of equal rank, forming what media wags eventually dubbed the "College of Cardinals." The analogy was fitting!

The hypothesis gains most of its credibility from the even pattern of factional alternations of the presidency and of the army minister (the "watchdog") throughout the 1967 to 1979 period. President Costa e Silva, a hard-liner, named General Lyra Tavares, a moderate, as army minister. Illness ended the second general-president's term at about midpoint in his five-year tenure, and presented the ruling junta and High Command with a perplexity. The "agreement" seemed to call for naming another hard-liner as the successor, and General Médici very aptly filled that niche, having been a personal protégé and chief of staff to Costa e Silva on two or three previous occasions, and having been a cabinet officer as head of the intelligence service, SNI. He therefore came from an eminently authoritarian assignment, especially appropriate in view of the serious guerrilla menace the country then faced.

Continuing with the pattern, Médici named another moderate, Orlando Geisel, as his army minister. The latter had a hand in delivering the presidential succession to his younger brother, Ernesto Geisel, whose credentials as a moderate were unquestionable. The latter, as the fourth general-president, chose Dale Coutinho to be army minister. Coutinho, a staunch hard-liner, died in that office the same year and he was succeeded by Sylvio Frota, another good hard-liner, who likewise did not complete the presidential term, having been dismissed—a serious incident to be further discussed below. President Geisel, in taking the ultimate risk upon himself, was careful to appoint a third hard-line general, Fernando Belfort Bethlem, to complete the reminder of his term as army minister.

If there is a flaw in the pattern, it would be in regard to classification of the final military president and his head of the army bureaucracy. João Figueiredo could have as easily been categorized as a moderate, considering his close ties to the ESG and to its "gray eminence," General Golbery, under whose tutelage Figueiredo had quickly risen to senior positions. Figueiredo was also an intellectual—more aptly ascribed to moderates than to the field commanders who generally hewed to the hard line—having been the top scholar in his cadet, junior officer (ESAO) and midcareer staff college (ECEME) classes: the rare "triple crown." However, he had his quota of field commands, and he came to the presidency from that key post of the hard line, director of the SNI. If it matters that much, at least the press chose to label Figueiredo a hard-line member. His army minister was Walter Pires, who in many ways also was an ambiguous quantity in terms of labels. Pires had a good career record in field commands, but he was a graduate of the ESG, and he was one of those whom President Geisel promoted from beneath other eligible generals. By such criteria, he was apt to be regarded as having been drawn out of the moderate ranks.

Aside from the regularity of the above pattern, the way the High Command in 1969 and the President in 1977 handled special circumstances while abiding in general terms by the agreement further bears out the essential validity of the hypothesis. For almost two months, amid growing speculation but no announcement, the temporarily ruling army–navy–air force junta delayed making a formal statement about the successor, and then summoned Congress from its eleven-month recess to ratify their choice. Why such a lengthy delay, one might well ask? Was it a pseudodemocratic ritual of balloting or canvassing lower ranks' preferences, as several analysts (Schneider 1971; Flynn 1979) from afar speculated? There could hardly have been a more urgent occasion for haste in returning to a pseudolegitimate presidency, amid the panic made evident in the rapid capitulation to guerrilla demands for the release of the fifteen most notorious radical prisoners in ransom for their kidnapped hostage, U.S. Ambassador Burke Elbrick. In fact, Médici had been obviously "selected" as Costa e Silva's successor for nearly two weeks—relieved after only a few months as Third Army commander in his native Rio Grande do Sul state and brought to Brasilia for no other recognizable purpose. It seems clear that consultations with the rest of the High Command continued through the latter half of September and part of October over resolution of an entirely different matter than the issue of who would be the next president. Initially reluctant to serve as successor, Médici temporarily stymied the seniors of the military elite with his demand that he have a complete, five-year term, if he became the next president. That was a powerfully controversial question, in that the plans of likely aspirants to be the next president—due next to a moderate such as Army Minister Orlando Geisel—depended upon not having run past the inflexible twelve-years-as-general ruling which had been put in place immediately after the 1964 coup, as an impediment to the military "empire-building" practices then being practiced. Plans had to be carefully guided on fixed paths, in part because of another standing rule: only active duty four-star generals should become president!

If we can presume that the difficulty with General Medici's demand for a full term was reluctantly swallowed, it does not tax the imagination much to reason that Army Minister Orlando Geisel had obtained the assurance that the succession would go to his younger but already eligible brother, Ernesto—much like Costa e Silva, who had bargained in 1965 for the guarantee that he would be Castello Branco's successor. As one should thereby expect, the nomination of Ernesto Geisel five years later to be the fourth army president was accepted without a sign of opposition.

Next let us consider the October 1977 crisis, when President Geisel seemingly abandoned his obligation to allow the opposite faction to retain primacy over the army hierarchy as army minister. This tough decision was taken after it became clear that General Frota not only aimed to be the next nominee for the presidency, but was unwilling to abide by the congressional edict prohibiting active campaigning for the office until six months prior to the next election, which would be in November 1978. In this, Frota was supported by a number of dissidents in the progovernment ARENA party, as well as by a sizable backing among his army colleagues whom he had assiduously courted from the time he became minister. Details of the democratic reopening process are discussed in a subsequent chapter; but when Frota openly flouted rules on political behavior, President Geisel drew on a large if silent reserve of conservative supporters. Thus, though his actions were risky, in breaching the agreed pattern of alternations (which he in fact respected by his next choice for army minister), the ultimate choice staring the High Command members in the face was either to oust a sitting president, or to allow the president his day. Actually, cabinet ministers in ordinary circumstances serve at the pleasure of the president, so the choice—in view of Frota's indiscretions and insubordination—was fairly obvious.

Before returning to the military elite's solutions to the factionalism problem, and the correlation of events with the indications drawn from my survey of elite ideologic attitudes, one more facet of this hypothesized alternation agreement should be noted. In relatively concurrent studies of the Brazilian character, Lloyd Free (1961) and Hadley Cantril (1965) each noted the unique capacity of the Brazilian people to achieve compromise in the face of any threat of violence. Free even suggested that, if all nations could somehow be infused with the Brazilian character, it would mean the end of wars. If that sounds like hyperbole, one should recall the climactic hours on the March 31, 1964 political-military crisis, when two regiments might well have met in battle, starting a civil war. At the very time that the First Army leader, sent out to intercept and attack the rebel regiment led by General Mourão Filho, should have been engaging in mortal combat he instead merely camped and waited to see which way the São Paulo–based Second Army commander chose to turn—rebellion or loyalty to Goulart. Then, with the issue settled, he joined up with Mourão Filho's troops, returning to Rio de Janeiro (then the de facto capital) in a "victory march." The incident was not unique; in fact many such incidents could be cited to illustrate Brazilians' characteristic reluctance to force an issue, if some meaningful compromise to engaging in combat could be achieved.

Differentiating Several Attitudinal Cluster Groups

Thus far, discussion has centered upon the two most important and diametrically opposite factions of the armed forces: the so-called "hard-liners" and the "moderates." Their views on internal security policy and external affairs, as they related to national development policy, marked them as belonging, respectively, to the "authoritarian nationalist" and "democratic internationalist" factional groups. As cited earlier, there were additional, recognizable attitudinal groups. One group, which Riordan Roett (1972: 95, 154ff) described as the "legalists," took a nationalist view of Cold War issues, opposing Brazil's tilt current toward the West. Peter Flynn (1979: 239, 253–55, 274) called that faction "democratic nationalists." Though I find no exact references to an "authoritarian internationalists" group, one can readily imagine that there have to have been essayists reflecting a body of opinion within the elite that was "authoritarian" regarding internal subversive threats and communism in general and who favored capitalist models (thus, "pro-West") in their attitudes about national development policy. The four groups thus identified become, logically, equatable to the polar positions on the scaling of attitudes toward internal security and international relations.

Thinking ahead to the means to analyze data from the same survey of essay literature dealt with in chapter 3, we have two dependent variables, internal security policy and international relations policy, affecting national development policy, our independent variable. Clearly it would be helpful to simplify the data base, in what would otherwise become a multivariable analysis. Ithiel de Sola Pool's "building blocks" concept (1959: 203) for manipulation of multiple variables in content analysis of communications, much like Alfred Stepan's (1971: 102) suggested "attitudinal clusters," served the purpose very well.

A scatter plot analysis for each of the five periods gave additional clarity to the above-suggested organization by cluster groups. Plotting degrees of expressed concern for internal security policy on the ordinal axis—high, medium, low, or nil, as scaled in the preceding chapter at values of 3, 2, 1, and 0, respectively—made up one parameter of these plots. The abscissa, representing attitudes about international affairs, was also scaled as before: nationalist views were plotted at -1, neutrals (nil) at 0, pro-West at $+1$, and pro–United States at $+2$. If there had been evidence of a pro-East (i.e., socialist) ideology on development policy, it would have been scaled at -2. As pointed out earlier, this viewpoint did not emerge in my survey of military professional essay literature.

Since the objective was to accurately portray factional lines of significant policy differences, the final question was where to place the dividing lines between the four cluster groups. On the ordinal scale, the division between authoritarians and those of a relatively democratic mind was taken at midpoint, so that a low or negligible score on internal security policy received the label as "democratic," and the high and medium-scaled scores marked an essayist as "authoritarian." On the international relations axis, it seemed clear that essayists scored as "nationalist" were distinct from any scored as neutral (negligible). Likewise, those essayists scored as pro-West could be grouped with those scored as pro–United States, compatibly regarded as "internationalists." The five scatter plots, thus divided, left a fairly small fifth group with neutral views on East-West or nationalist-internationalist policy toward national development, which could be regarded as neutrals. I omitted from further consideration, but nonetheless included those in the mean score computations for each period.

Aggregating and Testing the Cluster Groups

The principal question is whether each of the four groups held significantly different attitudes toward national development policy. Put methodologically, the null hypothesis is that, for each period, no significant differences in attitudes toward development policy existed between the four groups. Analysis should be extended longitudinally over each of the same five-year intervals—because the composition of the cluster groups can be assumed to vary, period by period, not only due to new policy directions that different presidents and their advisers introduced, but also due to external influences. The comparative sizes of the four groups, and how each group's attitudes may have been influenced by leadership decisions and current development policy as Brazil moved through each period, is a further matter of interest.

Various statistical methods were tried; in making the initial test of the validity of the null hypothesis, the best methods were found to be the simple analysis of variance test (F test) and Kolmogorov's goodness of fit test (D statistic). By the former, F ratios (i.e., mean squares of scores between groups, to mean squares within the group) in the 60 to 100 range or more were consistently beyond the.05 significance level. Kolmogorov's D test also bore out the validity of the cluster divisions, producing criteria of significance at the.01 level (i.e., randomly occurring in one of a hundred cases) for sixteen of the twenty cases, to justify rejection of the null hypothesis. The clusters also proved valid internally, each differentiating significantly coherent attitudes toward national development policy. The aggregate scores of the four cluster groups on development policy were then tested against the mean development score of the entire population for each of the five-year periods. Because of its higher discriminating powers where relatively large numbers are included in the testing universe, the Kolmogorov D statistic was adopted for use in subsequent analyses. In table 4.1 below, the sizes of the

Table 4.1.
Group Scores on Development Policy Attitude Scale

	Years				
	1963	1968	1973	1978	1983
Aggregated scores[a]	(81)1.83	(88)1.96	(82)1.49	(78)1.88	(88)1.64
Authoritarian Nationalists	(10)1.80[b]	(26)2.27	(19)2.05	(13)2.15	(21)1.76[c]
Authoritarian Internationalists	(20)0.45	(12)1.58	(2)1.00	(5)1.60	(2)0.50
Democratic Nationalists	(29)2.69	(21)2.33	(31)1.84	(28)2.18	(42)2.07
Democratic Internationalists	(9)1.22	(25)1.72	(12)1.33[d]	(13)1.46	(17)0.82

a Aggregated scores on development attitude included essayists of the "neutrals" cluster group.

b Kolmogorov D for this group was nonsignificant.

c Kolmogorov D for this group was significant at the .20 level.

d Kolmogorov D for this group was significant at the .10 level.

For every other group, the level of significance equalled or exceeded the .01 level.

respective cluster groups are indicated within parentheses for each period, just ahead of the group's development policy score.

The most unexpected finding in the overall analysis was that, with the exception of 1968, the size of the "democratic nationalist" group exceeded the sizes of the more publicly recognized attitudinal groups, the "authoritarian nationalists" and the "democratic internationalists." More will be said below about this finding. The growing strength of each of the two "nationalist" groups, as well as the drift away from policies favoring collaboration with the United States and the capitalist West, are other striking revelations. Whereas in 1963 and 1968 the margin of nationalists (of both groups) over those labeled as internationalists (two groups) was small, the ratio became as much as 3.5 to 1 in 1973, and remained nearly as large thereafter. Corroborations of these findings on the basis of the professional literature authored by the military elite can be found in many experts' accounts of Brazil's relations with the United States and the West, and of its demonstrated interest in extending its commerce and political relations into China, the Soviet Union, and many nations such as the Arab states of the nonaligned bloc.

In reviewing table 4.1 and notes taken with the reviewing of essays published in 1963 and 1968, which were the only periods in which there was a significant cluster group of authoritarian internationalists, it seems clear that those authors' views had been very much affected by the phenomenon of Castroism, and fears that violent class struggle might soon begin to spread within their country. The table further indicates that this particular group exhibited very low interest in the national development issue area, compared with other groups. As the data suggests, after the marked success of the 1968–1971 campaign against urban guerrillas, this group shrank to insignificance. Democratic nationalists, on the other hand, grew steadily in relative size, and consistently demonstrated highest or next-highest concern on matters of development strategy and national policy-making.

EVOLUTIONARY TRENDS IN FACTIONAL POLICY DIFFERENCES

When the Castello Branco regime came into office, it brought in not only some of the top civil-military leadership recruited from the alumni and faculty lecturer associates of the ESG—the "Sorbonne" to its devoted disciples—but it also imposed various "school solutions" to often-studied problems of regional and national development. It also sharply reversed the policy of the prior administration, which had emphasized national rather than international entrepreneurship, losing in the process much momentum and overseas investors' confidence. The leadership did not seem aware that, even among the military elite, its pro-Americanism and developmental ideology did not enjoy very broad support. Another trait that did not endear the *Castellista* regime to much of the military elite was its manifest disinterest in engaging in public ceremonial affairs, in the established tradition of all prior national leaders. There was also dismay, especially among authoritarian nationalists, over the great extent to which the first military leadership was guided not by top military brass, but by civilian technocrats, intellectuals, and politicians.

It is important to note that the Brazilian governments, from 1964 through the five successive presidencies, relied at least as much for important policy decisions upon senior civilian elites as upon top-level military leaders, once the High Command had made its choice of successors to the presidency. In concentrating in this investigation on ways that military leaders made and carried out development policy, the important roles played by civilian bureaucrats, politicians, and even nongovernmental academic and industrial elites tends to be overlooked. Those much more numerous policy instigators and advocates have always been a factor of real, but typically unmeasured, importance in the military's attempts to carve out new paths for Brazil's development progress, or to generate fresh impetus to former programs and strategies.

Internal Security Concerns

By examining table 4.1, there is convincing evidence that the internal security concerns of the two groups we have labeled "authoritarian" correlate negatively with expressed interest in national development policy matters. Authoritarian internationalists continually scored lower on development policy attitude than the democratic internationalists (*Castellista* group), sometimes by a very large margin. Likewise, with a small exception in 1973, democratic nationalists measured higher than authoritarian nationalists (*Costista* group), and in the 1963 and 1983 periods by a large margin, a trend that was also true of both internationalist groups.

Unlike the authoritarian internationalists, dismissed as insignificant after 1968, the authoritarian nationalist group did not decline appreciably in the 1970s and 1980s periods. They had the potential for institutional or personal self-interest, but it seems fair to say that they also believed that any relaxation of internal security might soon be followed by a return of guerrilla activism. A review of research notes from my survey reveals that, if they were inclined to say much about the resultant impact upon national development, it was to point out that renewed efforts to combat the guerrilla menace would entail an unacceptable risk of losing the hard-won development progress of recent years. The reexamination of my notes also revealed that a sizeable majority—on the order of five to one—of the authoritarian nationalist group after 1968 were scored as showing medium rather than high concerns over the internal security issue. Army authors dominated in that cluster group. These added insights convince me that differences of opinion about internal security between nationalists and internationalists did not separate and affect development policy-making. Once the Médici regime appeared to have overcome the guerrilla threat, the democratic authoritarians advocated a fairer wage policy, as a major step in neutralizing the issue of capitalist injustice toward the poor working class. They seemed to appreciate, more than authoritarians, the greater durability of an internal order that was not imposed and enforced, but obtained within a citizenry that saw possibilities of dialogue, social progress, and a fairer and ultimately more equitable opportunity for ambitious individuals.

Divisions over International Relations

The Castello Branco government believed that the primary obstacle that had held Brazil back, aside from inept and corrupt politicians, was the general lack of investment. In this opinion, they were echoed (or perhaps prompted) by North American economic think tanks such as Business International, which concluded (1965: 1) that the chief development barrier thus far limiting the "stumbling giant" was "lack of capital in the broadest sense of the word." Though the country had perennially suffered serious shortages of machinery, all manner of technical know-how, and working capital, the most urgent needs were "roads, port facilities, electricity, water, food, housing, educational facilities, and much equipment." Those needs were high on the list of development projects that the government was anxious to begin, and it was then a noteworthy U.S. commitment under the Alliance for Progress plan to fund such plans and support them with technical assistance. At the same time, at least until 1967, the government was committed to drastic reduction in the rate of inflation through austere fiscal practices and wage limitations—antithetical though that effort would be to rising public spending for projects initiated throughout the country.

Some of the actions taken might have gained wider public support, had it not been for the austere wage and price policies used to combat inflation. The new National Housing Bank, for example, made a positive start on addressing the serious housing shortage. With restored creditworthiness, loans were made available for small and midsized industries through the National Development Bank, also new. Other new funds were created to help finance purchases of heavy capital equipment and, in an unusual effort to stimulate capitalism among middle-class Brazilians, a form of payroll tax called FUNDECE (Fund to Democratize Capital), which encouraged employees to save by purchasing shares in their companies. Less well-accepted measures included temporary abolition of wage adjustments for inflation and the relaxation of profit remittance regulations imposed in 1962—plainly intended to encourage an influx of European and American investments, which soon followed. For many years, Brazil had not been as profitable as many other countries in terms of returns on investments.

The first government achieved a great deal by getting a depressed economy on an upward path while addressing the rampant inflation—less successfully than financial theories would have predicted—on this issue, protagonists of both right and left, and the "hardline" faction as well, saw the Castellista group as wrong-headed and antinationalistic. To Business International (1965: 2) the achievements were commendable. The government was doing "everything politically feasible" to gain capital investments, which it regarded as the "only way Brazil can get enough . . . to start an era of sound expansion." Milder praise came from Thomas Skidmore (1973: 31) who doubted that new policies such as those initiated by the Castello Branco government, in view of the "animus against the export sector" . . . under the influence of the ECLA [i.e., "dependency] thesis," could have been sold by an elected government. But the notion that Brazil was being "sold out" to foreign, especially American, bidders, was more prevalent. Miguel Arrães (1972: 170–71) saw the Castello Branco government as "pro-imperialist," declaring: "Undeniably, the regime's fundamental aim is integration with the United States. Given the economic and technical superiority of the United States, integration means in actual fact subordination of the Brazilian economy to North American imperialist interests." Yet, for Arrães (1972: 169), then living in exile in Algeria, there was no great difference between the Castello Branco and Costa e Silva regimes, which he declared to be "in perfect unity in their pursuit of the objectives laid down for them."

It can hardly be disputed that there were real differences in both ideology and policy initiatives between the first government and those of Costa e Silva and his protégé-successor (Médici); even though lengthier and more objective perspectives are necessary to see what they were. Even though the inflation rate had remained stuck in the 30 to 40 percent range when Costa e Silva took over, he determined that wage-price controls should be monetarily adjusted. His government also decided to impose more control over the twenty-two states (in a federal system where a governor had more "clout" and patronage possibilities than federal authorities), initiating a revenue rebate plan for both state and municipal levels, but at the same time denying them independent revenue sources through customs, excise, sales, and transfer tax collections, which had been their principal sources of revenue. Certainly those practices can be criticized as regressive in their impact upon domestic economic growth and freedom, but it seems evident that centralization and control were the real objectives. The rates of revenue shared were tied to those collected from each state—and thence parceled out on a comparable basis to municipal populations by the states—initially at a ratio of 10 percent, starting in 1967. This share was cut to 7 percent the next year, partially out of anticipated fiscal stringencies, but more so out of recognition that the funds were enabling uncontrolled spending on unplanned pet projects of local bosses. A Federal Tribunal of Accounts was expected to begin monitoring and restricting local abuses, but it was too undermanned—and possibly too easily also corrupted—to serve the purpose. Subsequently, the rate was again cut to 5 percent.

Tax evasion has always been a common problem, in Brazil and in much of the Third World, because of deficient public administration and—naturally, because of the easy opportunities—widespread corruption by both taxpayers and collectors. One of the first areas addressed under the Alliance for Progress was to assist Brazilian revenue authorities in undertaking a complete overhaul of the tax collection system, notably for the first time placing record keeping and data processing on computers. Costa e Silva was thereby presented with a "golden calf" of previously unimagined proportions. Siegel (1973: 375) noted that federal tax collections increased, in constant value terms, by 40 percent between 1961 and 1967. Robert Moss (1972: 28) found that, in São Paulo state alone, the number of taxpayers rose from just over 200,000 in 1967, to 2,700,000 three years later!

The second military government effectively combined a "carrot and stick" approach to revenue processes: generous tax concessions permitted individuals to deposit designated sums ranging from 10 to 25 percent of the income tax due into public investment banks such as those for tourism, fisheries, and national industries, receiving stock certificates for deposits. These allowed the patron to redeem the stock certificate, in some cases as soon as several years later. In one year alone, according to Siegel (1973: 124), the new entrants into "stock market" types of investment savings numbered more than one million.

Corporate taxation incentives were even more generous, being linked with governmentally controlled regional development plans. The faltering SUDENE program for resurrecting the depressed northeast region got a strong boost with corporate tax payments of as much as 50 percent diverted to investments in the company's name. The northern region (Amazônia) had a similar organization, SUDAM, with equivalent corporate taxes directed its way. Subsequently, with alternate tax diversions being directed toward reforestation and the faltering fishing industry, SUDENE and SUDAM were adversely affected.

Strangely, the relaxations of fiscal and taxation policy to wage earners and to corporations did not heat up the economy. In fact, inflation actually declined to the 20 to 30 percent range by 1969, and did not start upward for another few years. By 1968, meanwhile, the economic rate of growth reached 10 percent, and remained at that level or higher—peaking in 1971 at 11.8 percent, exceeding every other country of the industrial world—until by 1975 global recession and the heavy outflow of money for oil imports curbed the "miracle growth years."

Foreign investments continued to enter Brazil apace throughout the Costa e Silva and Médici administrations, seeming to conflict with the nationalist ideology which was to have been ushered in with the next government. Actually, the second government's policy was little different in regard to investors from the European and North American continents. In matters of economic strategy, both the second and third military regimes were content to leave this area to their young wizard, Antônio Delfim Neto, who had been launched upon his government career by Castello Branco, who first appointed him to be economic secretary for São Paulo state and then—after brilliant success in righting the affairs of that crucial state—to an economic planning role in Brasilia. As Skidmore (1988: 68–69) pointed out, Delfim was neither pro-American nor nationalist in basic philosophy, but a pragmatist anxious to obtain maximum gain from whatever sources. Since he was carried over for the five-year term under President Médici, and since the economy of Brazil bloomed so wondrously under his care, those of the nationalist persuasion were left in want of a cause and champion in high governmental circles.

The Médici government, buoyed by the rising national economy and growing availability of tax revenues, lost little time in embarking upon ambitious development projects such as the network of hydroelectric dams, basic industries such as iron and steel mills, and the "interiorization" of the development effort by the dramatic TransAmazon Highway project. To some extent, these were demonstrations of a different, more nationalistic ideology. Nevertheless, critics (exclusively Brazilian) attacked such long-range, expensive projects as "Pharaonic" monuments to ego. Less criticism accompanied three programs with social rather than infrastructural emphases: the land tenure reform measure, PROTERRA; the recomposition of the hodgepodge welfare system under Social Integration System (PIS); and the plans for tying together much of the transport and communications systems in a Program of National Integration (PIN). Whereas the industrial sector was forging for itself newly independent, promising opportunities in world markets, the good fortunes of the times were turning attention in Brasilia to some of the nation's pressing social ills and overdue reform measures. But even though the rhetoric of Médici and his ministers was nationalistic—and well received—the methods chosen remained highly authoritarian.

With internal security no longer a pressing issue by the time Ernesto Geisel assumed the presidency in March 1974, economic policy was about to become the centerpiece and potentially dividing issue area. Importation of more than 75 percent of Brazil's oil needs at ever-escalating prices soon drove minor policy matters from the scene, as the new president—just departed from the huge state corporation, PETROBRAS—assumed centralized direction of his government's economic policies. Though Geisel was unquestionably a moderate, he was far less an internationalist than his now deceased mentor, Castello Branco. In fact, PETROBRAS had always been the focal point of Brazilian economic nationalism, ever since the mid-fifties era when it was created with the rallying cry of "The oil is ours!" He had inherited an administration permeated with the preoccupation of strong export emphasis, and it was an obvious imperative by the mid-seventies that this emphasis must continue, if Brazilian importation costs—not only for oil but for its flourishing industries—were to be covered.

Though there were many continuities from the third military regime to the fourth under Geisel, one of the most significant differences was the absence from center stage of Antônio Delfim Neto as minister of finance. His office was taken over by the astute but much more conventional conservative, Mario Henrique Simonsen. The Planning Ministry, which later became the focal point of strategy formulation, remained in the hands of João dos Reis Velloso, an economist who had served in the government since 1964. Geisel continued to follow an independent borrowing policy, eschewing ties to the IMF in those years when Brazil was able to keep well ahead of its creditors in direct loans from European, Japanese, and American banks. However, he foresaw harsher years because the reserves of foreign exchange and fiscal liquidity were rapidly declining. Future petroleum purchases were unavoidable, and fuel conservation could not relieve the impact on the treasury while awaiting reprieves from the development of grain alcohol substitutions in motor vehicles (from biomass, chiefly sugar cane) and hydroelectric power dams and nuclear power plants under construction.

The one uncharacteristic Geisel decision, which might have been advocated earlier by his moderate (i.e., democratic internationalist) faction, and still enjoyed partisan support, was the May 1975 plan to offer petroleum exploration "risk contracts" to foreign companies, seeking thereby to obtain more domestic fuel sources. By the mid-seventies, however, public opinion and a sizable portion of Congress saw this as inimical to national security, and reacted vigorously to this proposal to admit intrusions into a national preserve. In the end, only three such contracts were issued under closely restricted regional controls and, as Skidmore (1988: 208) noted, none of them found petroleum deposits. Where Standard Oil in the early 1950s had likewise struck out, perturbing rabid nationalists who for a time charged that the Americans were hiding their findings to later exploit Brazil's resources for their own profit, now antagonists of the risk contract project received the news without surprise and perhaps even with suppressed glee.

Other measures furthering national interests were initiated during the Geisel administration, heavily concentrated in the petroleum industry. To add impetus to the growing field research aspects of PETROBRAS—excluding intensive searches in offshore areas found to be more promising than inland oil explorations—PETROQUISA was spun off, to devote its efforts to energy conservation research. BRASPETRO became another spinoff for intensified drillings and explorations. Likewise, distribution aspects came under PETRODIS, who, having previously begun building grain tankers, now moved into construction of large oil tankers, while the task of optimizing negotiations for petroleum on the world market was given to another subsidiary, INTERBRAS. Finally the PROALCOOL program and bureau were created to promote conversions to alcohol fuel consumption.

Two badly handled and frankly interventionist policies on the part of the United States led to bad feelings on the part of Brazilians, including with few exceptions senior military officials. The U.S. Congress, by a 1976 law, began to require a statement on the record on human rights abuses by each country to which U.S. military assistance was being given. In 1977, based upon recorded past incidents, Brazil's status in the area of human rights behavior was reported in unfavorable terms, barely taking into account the improved environment of the current era. Incredibly, that report was distributed to Brazil's military commanders! Reacting in hurt and outrage, all ties between Brazil and the United States on military assistance—which had been of little importance for several years—were abruptly severed.

The second incident involved behind-the-scenes machinations between the United States and West Germany, seeking to prevent transfer of fissionable reactor core material for three and eventually as many as six nuclear power reactors, because Brazil was demurring on committing itself (along with Argentina and Cuba) to the Nonproliferation Treaty and the hemispheric Nuclear Free Zone (Tlatelolco) Treaty. Dependency theory spokespersons now had an ideal issue to exploit, and anti-Americanism soon grew among former friends among the officer corps, as Skidmore (1988: 196–97), Black (1980: 633), and Wesson (1982: 69–72) have noted. To Brazilians, there seemed to be less room for the old friendship now that the country had matured.

The Figueiredo government exhibited almost exactly the same attitude toward the United States and the West as its predecessor, not notably friendly but certainly correct and even cordial, yet much of the time embroiled in difficult negotiations for better terms on loan repayment schedules and improvements in trade and financial relations. In view of the debt issue, and after the setbacks of the past few years,—and with both nations at this point stern competitors in such varied external trade markets as agricultural products (not only tropical products but sugar, cotton, soybeans, grains, and citrus fruits and juices), iron and steel, and even manufactured goods—little more than this could be expected. Having cranked up a monumental and remarkably successful drive to export whatever it could, to whomever would buy, Brazilians had no particularly compelling reason to reserve special affection and courtesy for the United States and its current policies. When it became necessary to humble themselves, after nearing default by the end of 1982, and seek debt repayment concessions from the IMF—which in some minds was only an agency for western bankers, and thus by proxy for the U.S. government–inevitably anger grew within the military elite and the general public. The standard policy of the IMF, applied now to Brazil, meant an imposition of austerity upon an already impoverished lower-class majority, and threatened the fewer middle-class Brazilians with descent into the same levels of living standards and social circumstances.

Much more of the story of this period, involving the battle for fiscal survival, an industrial and agricultural productive growth born of adversity that was as remarkable as the "miracle growth" of a decade earlier, and the intricate politics by which ruling power was transferred to a civilian government, are left to subsequent chapters. It may have been adversity that brought ideologically divided factions to the collective view, widely but not unanimously shared, that it was now time to leave the policy-making business to politicians, and avoid the looming possibility of a collapse of armed forces unity. It was by no means clear that divisions were more serious by 1983 than they had been five or ten years earlier. But what was now becoming clear was the realization that the national enterprise faced harder times—times that promised little reward for those stalwarts who would next shoulder the burden of governing.

CONCLUSIONS

By aggregating and correlating the national development policy attitudes of the military elite according to four distinct ideologic cluster groups, we have identified one of the troublesome problems with which the military hierarchy had to deal over the 1964 to 1985 period. There was more unity at the outset, when different factions sensed the national crisis of policy drift (toward communism, as many feared); and there was considerable unity also by 1983, when the leadership and thoughtful essayists appeared to prefer relinquishment of power to continuing what by then appeared to be an unfair and unpromising developmental task.

A glance at table 4.1 is sufficient to reveal the difference in viewpoint toward development policy between internationalists and nationalists. The latter were, on weighted average, nearly twice as concerned as the internationalists, in the essay literature I surveyed, over how the national development policy was pursued. Internal security policy, on the other hand, did not ever carry as much importance in the literature as the international views (especially the dependency issue); after the apparent defeat of guerrilla groups by 1971, that issue area nearly vanished. There were almost no advocates of the "authoritarian internationalist" faction by 1973! Those who retained a demonstrated concern over international encroachment on Brazilian domestic industrial success, and also continued to warn against too rapidly liberalizing internal security controls, mostly belonged to the burgeoning intelligence apparatus, centered around the SNI, which was the last redoubt of the slowly diminishing hard-liner faction. But the survey shows that there were far more "democratic nationalists" by 1973 than "authoritarian nationalists," and by 1983 the ratio had climbed to two to one.

The differences in ideologic attitudes between the two most influential factions (moderates, identified also as democratic internationalists, and hard-liners, known here as authoritarian nationalists), were resolved without overt signs of rupture after the "coup within the Coup" of October 1965, through what I hypothesized and circumstantially substantiated as an "alternation agreement." This, with nearly precise regularity, permitted rotation of the presidency between moderates and hard-liners until 1979, at which point one could argue that the differences were more personal than ideological. It certainly helped, in any event, that the qualifications and character of João Figueiredo were such that on either side of the blurred dividing line, all but a few might claim the last president as being one of their own faction.

The conclusion supported by my literature survey of ideologies is that there was indeed a clear basis, at least through the first decade of military rulership, for the oft-cited cleavage between moderates and authoritarians in the military elite. When economic fortunes ran strongest (i.e., the early 1970s) and the Médici regime was acting more repressively than disinterested observers considered acceptable, divisions between factions also ran deeper. Then, when adversity loomed largest, in the form of heavy outlays for petroleum and the staggering debt repayment burden, the elite tended to close ranks, caring less about ideology (which was by then almost entirely nationalist) than about means of survival and resumption of economic development. Brazilians' characteristic resourcefulness and success at compromise emerges in this survey as one of their strongest personal assets.

5

New Directions for Development Strategy

Economic development in Third World countries in the last half of the twentieth century has been a delicate and uncertain process. For Brazil, the problems and complexities for government strategists are particularly challenging. It is appropriate to consider some of those problems before examining the chosen strategy of the military regimes. Brazil's great size, unlike China or India—the only two comparable cases—includes a much larger undeveloped and even unexplored interior, but nevertheless involves similar obstacles to economic development attributable to regional dissimilarities.

The nearly demographically vacant Amazon region is unlike any other territory in the world. The semiarid northeast region might be compared to the less populated parts (half a century ago) of the American Southwest, or perhaps to less developed parts of Iran or Turkey. The western Pantanal zone of Mato Grosso, now divided into two states, is also unique: inundated seasonally, it is usable only for range-type grazing animals. Brazil's southern states could be compared to the less densely populated parts of central Europe. Rio de Janeiro can hardly be compared to any other city-state, with its grinding poverty alongside striking beauty on public display. And then there is São Paulo, which in the foreseeable future can be expected to exceed even Mexico City in its population and urban sprawl, and it will almost certainly continue to exceed it in productivity. São Paulo state, sometimes depicted as "Brazil's locomotive pulling twenty-one sleeping cars," by 1985 had achieved a gross domestic product (GDP) in excess of $76 billion, placing it well ahead of the GDPs of every Latin American country except Mexico.

As Jacques Lambert (1959) aptly put it, there are "two Brazils"; rich agrarian and industrial lands concentrated in the Rio–São Paulo–Belo Horizonte central triangle, and the remaining parts of the nation where poverty-level populations outnumber the rich by at least twenty to one. That situation poses a paradox for strategists and national development planners, since the disparity of wealth is not conducive to democracy. Under authoritarian rule there is too little basis for control over the population, inevitably resulting in weak internal security. However, by favorable concentrations of wealth and capital resources, a government could optimize capitalist growth prospects through ordinary investment policies. Brazil attempted to produce an economic growth spurt by such means, and to a great degree succeeded, but failed to reap long-term benefits because of the social and political flaws of an inequitable economic development strategy.

This chapter will consider Brazil's strategy for development under military rule and, in a general way, thereby attempt judgment of the capability of authoritarian systems to manage broad national economic growth processes. This effort also implicitly considers how well the applied strategies might have substantiated recent theories about the economic development process. Factors which hindered or contributed to national development will also be identified whenever possible. It should be noted that somewhat unique principles and ideas were applied by Brazil's military leaders and their technocratic aides. The principal development theories adopted by Brazil were the "leading industrial sector" strategy of Albert Hirschman (1958) and the "economic takeoff phase" policies of Walter Rostow (1964).

Two particular principles the generals and technocrats applied were designed to avoid hyperurbanization in the central triangle, and to switch from import-substitution industrialization (ISI) of prior years to an export-led strategy, especially of manufactured products. The ISI growth pattern had already led to rapid growth of industrial centers, most of all São Paulo and its "ABC" satellite cities (São Andre, São Bernardo, and São Caetano). Now military leaders worried that further concentrations of labor in the central region of the country might represent a serious security threat. President Goulart had planned to create just such a leftist "labor cover" as a barrier to military intervention in the event of a future political crisis. The decentralization strategy, however, had within it the seeds of potential failure, due to the economic costs of building the needed infrastructure in outlying areas, and the extra transportation costs once the new industries were in operation.

Nevertheless, economic policymakers laid out development plans based upon new urban "poles of development" in the states adjacent to São Paulo, Minas Gerais, and Guanabara (subsequently incorporated into the larger state of Rio de Janeiro), as well as a few in the north and northeast regions. Of course, those plans were well received by pro-government politicians in the Congress, especially those from the less-developed states which, not incidentally, were where the military government's support was concentrated. They also gave enthusiastic support to the initial plans to colonize Amazônia, once the TransAmazon Highway system was approved; many Brazilians have long held to an "El Dorado myth" concerning supposed marvels of riches to be discovered there.

SUBSIDIZED, STATE-CONTROLLED INDUSTRIALIZATION

The usual definition of "state-controlled" industries within a capitalist nation is a form of mixed enterprises whereby private capital is supplemented (often being exceeded) by national government investments. In the case of a federation such as Brazil, there will ordinarily be many mixed enterprises operated in states, federal territories, and major municipalities. At any level, private investors hold stock certificates representing their share of the enterprise's proceeds and directorship, while the role of the government consists normally of the appointment of directors to the controlling board proportionate to its share of capital. In practice, after the earliest stage, with the ongoing capital requirements for growth and technologic advancement beyond the means of most private investors, more and more of the actual control has shifted to the government. Proliferation of the state enterprise model in Brazil, and fiscal barriers posed by recession and fuel import charges, increasingly intervened in financial plans, and foreign investors became a major component. As Peter Evans (1979) has well illustrated, this "tri-pé" (three-legged) stance further eroded the capacity of Brazilian investors to have effective impact on important policy decisions.

Even though the largest state corporations, PETROBRAS and ELECTROBRAS, were started before 1964, the strategy of state-run enterprises was only given real emphasis in the 1970s, when the total of nationally owned enterprises was approximately six hundred. Even the Rio Doçe Valley (CVRD) steel company, begun in 1946, bears almost no resemblance today to its pre–1964 form of management. A basic principle of the development policy was to stress and if necessary to subsidize basic industries such as steel fabrication.

Planning and Development Policy-making

Discussion of development progress starts in this study with decisions and strategies begun in the 1970s during the Medici administration. The Castello Branco and Costa e Silva regimes prepared the way for sustained economic growth by their careful attention to measures intended to reduce monetary inflation, even though no fully satisfactory results came about before 1970. Then, with an expansionist rather than austere economic policy, Antônio Delfim Neto seemed to refute conventional inflation-damping theory. Miraculously, he cut inflation rates to 15 percent by 1972, while the national GDP was growing at more than 10 percent annually. In concurrently removing the threat of anti-government guerrillism, Brazil became one of the hottest prospects to receive the swelling "petrodollar" deposits of Western banks, resulting from the OPEC price escalations of crude oil exports. Thus was Brazil afforded one or two extra years of financial counterweight to the heavy expenses it bore for its own petroleum imports.

Policy instruments. Robert Moss (1972: 28–30) has identified five factors, in addition to inflation control, that contributed most to the economic boom of the early 1970s: maintaining foreign investor confidence, providing investment tax incentives, increasing nationwide savings practices, investing in critical infrastructure needs, and promoting national exports. He felt that the measures to instill and preserve foreign investor confidence probably had the greatest impact. Not only was there assurance of a stable and effective government in control, adding to Brazil's attractiveness as a consumer market and source of low-cost, readily trainable workers, but there was a sympathetic regime in charge. Among the nationalists, it seemed excessively sympathetic. Additionally, unlike any other Third World countries, Brazil had the "crawling peg" process of minidevaluations one to two months apart, by which almost no risk was encountered in daily monetary exchanges of currencies.

More extensive treatments will be given to the export incentive and infrastructure policy instruments. The other two factors—savings and tax investment incentives—were so intertwined they need to be treated jointly. Thus one gains insight into the means by which fiscal resources were made available to subsidize much of the industrialization outside the developed triangle of central Brazil. Personal income tax collections, which were very much undercollected until the mid–1960s revenue improvement steps had been perfected with a few years' experience and training of Brazil's public administrators, became the means to exponentially expand the numbers of investors in local stock markets, through a "fiscal fund 157" tax remissions system. Though the stock shares could be redeemed or reinvested three years later, this plan was successful not only in encouraging greater personal savings but also in introducing middle-class employees to stock markets as a method of building future savings.

The plans concerning corporate tax concessions were complex. Briefly, there were up to 50 percent tax remissions for investments in the two major regional superintendencies (where a governing council determined which investment programs should be funded), for Northeast and Amazônia development. Besides programs benefitting SUDENE or SUDAM, there were smaller concessions aimed at subsidizing reforestation or timberland conservation (up to 25 percent of taxes due) and tourism development (up to 8 percent). *Metas e Bases Para a Acão de Govêrno, 1970* (Goals and Foundations for Government Action), seems to be a suitable instrument for policy analysis in this study.

Metas e Bases planned to commit $700 million into the industrialization of the northeast region over the 1971–1974 period through the existing tax concessions system. An additional $1.7 billion would be granted to ministries and states and even to municipalities of that region, for direct support of economic growth. Industrial growth was given much more emphasis in the plan than agricultural development. In my far more extensive earlier study (1973) devoted to water resource policies for Northeast development, there was clear evidence of disinterest in agriculture as a vehicle for development at that time. That bias stemmed not only from the prior poor reputation of such programs, including misuses of funds creating scandals at the ministry level and below, but also because the bureaucracy of the Planning Ministry regarded industrial development as not only surer and quicker, but much more cost-beneficial. Thus, for the 1971–1974 period, investments to develop the region's agriculture were only expected to reach the small sum of $275 million. Politicians from outlying states and a minor element among the military elite wanted much more.

Beyond the specific regional development programs, the *Metas e Bases* plan called for government outlays for industrialization (including minerals) over the next four years of more than $4.6 billion (1970 values) (Republica do Brasil 1970: 187). Of that sum, about 40 percent was to be given toward mining and metallurgic development alone. Over a billion dollars was to be allocated specifically to iron and steel industrial development! Though partial credit for vastly improved income tax collections in the 1970s must be given to the splendid economic growth and to computerized tax accounting measures, these incentive programs certainly assisted and boosted the tax collection effort. Consider, for example, that in the state of São Paulo the net number of taxpayers grew from about 200,000 to more than 2.7 million between 1967 and 1970 (Moss, 1972: 28). The stock certificates program for individual taxpayers swelled the number of Brazilian stockholders to more than a million by 1970. They also boosted the rate of savings from about 10 percent of GDP in the late 1960s to more than 21 percent two years later. Certainly much can be said for Brazilians' financial planning and performance as a result of such incentive plans, but most of the credit for the success must be given to the inflation controls and monetary corrections systems that removed incentives to spend what was earned immediately and encouraged future financial savings.

Goal-setting and priorities. When the Médici administration produced its comprehensive national development plan for the 1970–1974 period, the world market price for petroleum was about three dollars per barrel, and Brazil was importing more than 250 million barrels each year, amounting to about 85 percent of its annual consumption of petroleum products. That plan was actually Brazil's first valid test of the practice of comprehensive state development planning, previous efforts being either of very brief and interrupted nature (Castello Branco and Costa e Silva) or developed but not fully implemented (Goulart and Kubitschek). Now, with a booming national economy, ambitious plans stood real possibilities of being executed.

Other industrial priorities spelled out in the 1970 national plan included chemicals (including petrochemicals) and fertilizers, and a variety of electrical, electronic, and mechanical manufactures. Automobile manufacturers, while not singled out in the plan, were experiencing a major expansion of demand at home, with long-range development plans envisioning production for export to some of their Latin American neighbors and, perhaps, markets in the more developed western world. Ford, Chrysler, and General Motors were making major investments aimed at cutting into Volkswagen's dominance in the Brazilian market. Toyota and Fiat also entered more tentatively into the production field. Shipbuilding, until recently limited to small coastal vessels and confined to one private builder CCN (Commerce and Navigation Company), was soon to become a major employer of scarce, technically qualified labor in the Rio de Janeiro area when contracts were awarded calling for new offshore oil rigs and bulk carriers. Ishikawajima of Japan joined with a Brazilian subsidiary, on the strength of new contracts, to build five or more 130,000-ton supertankers.

An idea of the pace being set for basic industries' growth can be gained by looking at new goal-setting and results as they applied to the iron and steel industry. With over one billion dollars invested in expansion of this industry, steel ingot production was expected to increase from about 5 to 7.7 million tons in the 1970–1974 period. However, in spite of achieving the 6-million-ton output in the first year of the new plan—approximately 11 percent growth—demand for steel grew by 12 percent or more (IBGE, 1972: 123). Moss (1972: 51) cited the increased demand for 1971 as 28 percent—indicative of the problems of incomplete industry-wide reporting of activity in prior years—but his data regarding anticipated longer-range demand forecasts by the National Steel Company (CSN), formed recently to better coordinate the industry's new National Iron and Steel Plan, agrees quite well with my data source, the Instituto Brasileiro Siderurgia. IBS (Brazilian Iron and Steel Institute), organized to prepare market surveys and facilitate government planning, predicted demand for steel to reach more than 15 million tonnage by 1980. CSN's new director, General Americo da Silva, was an army engineer specialist in industrial methods, equipping him to guide planning efforts if not also the participation of Brazil's forty or more small private steel companies. Subsequent plans for large-scale exportation of steel, by which Brazil would rise from twentieth place to tenth among world producers, elevated industry goals to a predicted plateau of 25 million tons by the mid–1980s.

Mining activities—explorations, production, and exportation in particular—were also to receive major governmental emphasis. Aside from petroleum production, the major effort was directed to iron mining and an urgent development of pelletization plants, to offset greater costs of shipping the ore abroad. Out of a net governmental investment of more than $1 billion, planners expected to more than double iron ore production and exportation, predicting goals of 50 million tons and 450 million U.S. dollars, respectively, for the next four-year period. In fact, iron ore exports actually exceeded the goal: calculations based upon InterAmerican Development Bank data (IDB, 1981: 448) adjusted to reflect 1970 values would indicate that nearly $1 billion was realized from iron ore exports over the 1970–1974 period.

The above discussions about plans and their consequences for a typical basic industry, steel and iron ore production, are representative of the way that other industries in Brazil had to race to keep up with domestic and export demands. Similar tales could be told regarding development of modern industrial capacities in cement, petrochemicals, textiles, electronics, gold and gems, and even wood products. Indicative of the trend, as Brazil sought to become a major world power through trade, was the fact that iron and steel became by 1971 second only to coffee in contribution to export earnings, moving at the start of the decade ahead of cotton and sugar as a leading export commodity (IBGE 1972: 179–80).

Because the act of setting priorities for governmental sponsorship of industrial development programs—either through direct investments, tax concessions, or such external market protections as quotas on imports or protective tariffs—was of such enormous consequence, not only for the product line under development consideration but for many with which it interfaced, a Council of Industrial Development with high level authority had to be created. The CDI, headed by the minister of Industry and Commerce, included five other cabinet-level ministers (Finance, Interior, Mines and Energy, Planning, and Armed Forces General Staff), the presidents of the three major lending institutions operated by the state (Central Bank, Bank of Brazil, and Economic Development Bank), and the presidents of the National Confederation of Commerce and of the National Confederation of Industry. This governing council, being of unwieldy size had eight or more project study groups at its disposal to screen and help evaluate the proposals.

Because of the scarcity of available private investment funds in proportion to the scope and scale of industrial growth proposed under the ambitious national plan of the 1970s, it was necessary for the government to undertake a major role in the organization of new industries. Thus the rapid growth of numerous state enterprises came to dominate Brazilian industrial structure. As an illustrative study, let us examine the major state and private firms engaged in iron and steel production.

The Iron and Steel Industry

Discussions above have indicated the importance of this basic industry, as well as some of its major components. Actually, the government's controlling mechanisms under the overall direction of the Minister of Mines and Energy break down into two consortia (holding companies with policy roles): MINEROBRAS for mineral exploration, new mine development, and research (further directed by the government's DNPM—National Department for Mineral Research), and SIDERBRAS, which oversees the iron and steel industry per se. With the latter comprising eight or more separate state-owned iron and steel companies, and several times that many in the mixed and private enterprise sectors, some discussion of structure within the industry becomes a preliminary necessity to closer examination of the aforementioned Rio Doçe Valley (CVRD) Company, which had become Brazil's major earner of foreign exchange.

Industry Organization. Brazil's four largest companies, in terms of capital and reserves, are all state-operated, although in the turmoil of financial stringencies in the 1980s, portions of those have been effectively traded in refinancings with overseas investors, especially Japan. Volta Redonda, renamed the National Steel Company (CSN), is still largest in capacity if not in net earnings, followed by COSIPA (São Paulo–owned), and USIMINAS (Minas Gerais, partially owned by Japanese investors). CVRD, most often known as Rio Doçe Valley Company, is a conglomerate corporation with special missions, and will be further investigated below as a special case study. Other state-run iron and steel companies are USIBA (Bahia), ACESITA (Itabira Special Steel Company), and two new state enterprises: AÇOMINAS and the Tuberão Steel Company. The latter, unique in that it was for the first time located in the seaport of Tuberão (Espirito Santo state)—where its ocean access for export could be advantageous, but necessitating its own steel railway—became a contentious competitor with AÇOMINAS (inland but closer to resources and industrial infrastructure then in place) at the point in the early 1980s when due to a global recession, demand for steel abroad suddenly bottomed out. Either or both became serious candidates for abandonment when Brazil's liquidity crisis of 1983 demanded wide slashing of budgetary allocations to state companies.

In addition to further state steel and iron companies, formed with local and foreign capital mergers to develop the huge potential of the Carajás fields of the Amazônian region in Pará state (and not being included here, since they had not begun producing in the years under military administration), there were a variety of both large and small private companies engaged in the steel industry. An interesting example was the Belgo-Mineira Company, the world's largest integrated steel mill using charcoal rather than coke, in that its competitivity was somehow preserved while South Korea, Japan, and other steel producers were defeating older processors with their high technology and modern equipment. On the darker side, Belgo-Mineira's labor-intensive methods, which depended upon nonrenewable resources such as the eucalyptus forests in their area, made them vulnerable to world competition if and when the military regime or its successor abandoned the repressive wage controls which had made their labor-intensive methods financially feasible.

In contrast to the many small private companies, however, the state enterprises were vastly larger and needed major capital inputs, which could only come from governmental or foreign multinational sources. Even before the 1970 expansion plan was about to begin, the initial five state enterprises engaged in steel production were several times larger in terms of capital assets than the five largest private steel producers. The latter were more productive. In terms of profits-to-assets ratios in 1969, they returned nearly 7 percent, compared with less than 6 percent from the five state corporations. If one deducted the huge earnings of the CVRD—then primarily engaged in iron ore sales, which enjoyed a banner year (contributing more than two-thirds of the profits of the state companies combined)—the other four state enterprises engaged in steel production only returned 2.3 percent profit. The one best situated, COSIPA in São Paulo, actually returned a net loss for that year (Business International, 1971: 87).

CVRD as a Case Study. The 1970 National Development Plan (*Metas e Bases* 1970: 197–98) directed about $750 million toward five "priority projects" to be achieved by CSN, USIMINAS, USIBA, COSIPA, and Aços Finos Piratini (a small mixed enterprise in Brazil's southernmost state), but made no plans to subsidize the Rio Doçe Valley Company (CVRD). In view of the excellent profits being earned, as indicated above, and the unconcern Brazil was feeling about trade balancing through exports emphasis in the years immediately preceding the 1973–74 OPEC actions in the oil market, this should not be surprising. Being semiautonomous (in the CVRD case, with no apparent need for government subsidy, fully independent), the state corporations were expected to operate in the black, and to reinvest earnings as the directorship chose, to meet its year-to-year operating costs and expansion requirements.

Until recessions struck much of the developed, market-oriented world in the late 1970s, iron and steel products were in great and growing demand worldwide. CVRD, being well positioned and showing ample profits—more than $50 million in 1969—could and did invest in iron and additional product lines. During the following decade, major developments under CVRD control were undertaken in some fields clearly within the iron and steel mandate of the Rio Doçe Valley Company, such as in geologic explorations, special ferrite minerals, and acquisition of a few small mining and mineral sales organizations. Other investments were aimed at a vertical product line integration (shipping, port facilities, repair facilities, and securities management services), and with market linkages to Italy, Spain, Japan, and the United States. The explosive reach of CVRD into diversified lines—not all as logical or profitable as the foregoing—can now be seen by Rio Doçe's satellite state enterprises in several aluminum companies, some forestry and cellulose companies, and even fertilizer company investments.

Toward the end of military rule, the official directory of the government, *Autoridades Brasileiras* (Empresa Brasileira de Noticias 1984: 120–24) showed no less than thirty subordinate companies under CVRD, maintaining offices in five states and the Federal District as well as six other countries (Belgium, Italy, Spain, Japan, the United States, and the Bahamas). At one point, CVRD was so encouraged by major sales to China that plans were in formative stages to charter another consortial enterprise to be named CHINABRAS. With so much linguistic and cultural know-how necessary to create an effective enterprise, the plan appeared unsound. Later, China backed out of renewal of the purchase orders, and in fact became a keen rival of Brazil particularly in the pig iron market.

As the 1970s neared an end, CVRD and its several state enterprise partners lumbered along on the ambitious plans to reach the 25-million-ton steel production capacity plateau cited above, hoping to exploit low worldwide investment in steel and an assumed marketing advantage by which to raise Brazil up to the top ten nations in terms of production. And in fact Brazil stood tenth with 15 million tonnage by 1980, when other countries such as the United Kingdom, Czechoslovakia, Belgium, Spain, and Romania, which had outproduced Brazil in prior years, had been overtaken. Productions of pig iron and of iron ore mining, in which Brazil already ranked among the top ten world producers, exhibited much the same pattern with both of those being areas in which CVRD had primacy in Brazil. For a world producer who was more dependent on petroleum imports than any other competitor except Japan, the achievements were remarkable. Equally remarkable was the blind adherence to timetables without regard to falling market demand. In time, of course, dire consequences were to be reaped when the OPEC oil producers decided in late 1979 to again double oil prices.

Over the period that began under the 1970 National Development Plan (*Metas e Bases* 1970: 207, 243), with a $7 million first allocation, CVRD and "another enterprise to be created," were given the controlling interest in the development of iron ore extraction and sales from *Grande Carajás*, in the Amazônian interior of the state of Pará. Here, within a 40-kilometer radius, was the largest concentration of high-grade iron ore in the world. With an estimated 66 percent of iron per ton, measured reserves of over a billion tons and estimated total reserves of 18 billion tons, Carajás was predicted to have as much as three times the iron ore available to the remainder of the world's producers (*Latin American Regional Reports, Brazil* RB 82–08: 4–5). Additionally, the region of *Grande Carajás*, conveniently near the huge Tucuruí hydroelectric complex, according to government (CPRM) and World Bank surveys held over a billion tons of copper reserves, 60 million tons of manganese ore, 40 million tons of bauxite, and valuable deposits of gold, nickel, cassiterite and other marketable minerals. Wood reserves for paper and building materials were also abundantly available, but mostly in the backwater area inundated for the Tucuruí dam; these were left to rot (and potentially to foul the dam's turbines later on) as a result of initial contract malfeasance and the haste to bring the electric potential on line.

U.S. Steel became the major capital provider along with CVRD in the Carajás iron mining venture at the start, with the two creating ITACO (Itabira International Company), and in time a subsidiary, Rio Doçe America. Escalating cost factors and capital contraction problems in U.S. Steel led to later decisions to bring in Japanese steel interests, managed by Nippon KK which was an overseas agent for several Japanese steel mills. In brief, though poor planning and financial administration bore some of the responsibility, the heart of the problem seems to have been in the remoteness of Carajás, with all of the assorted costs of development, the problems of ill-trained new personnel, and inadequate supervision. There were also major, one-time costs borne by the government: building an 890-kilometer access rail line out of the mine complex, and building the port facilities in Maranhão state at Ponta da Madeira, plus interim problems with transport costs on that railway. This leads to a further study of planning-execution mistakes worth recounting.

Due to the unexpected delay in bringing the Tucuruí Dam into service, and despite the now elevated costs for petroleum by 1980, CVRD had to resort to deisel-powered locomotive transport on its new rail line to Ponta da Madeira, rather than to utilize the eventually abundant electric power. Estimates ranging in the vicinity of two dollars per ton added to the cost of the iron ore delivered to ocean transport, meaning a 10 percent increase in sale price which certainly reduced profit, and quickly threatened Brazil's ability to market its iron ore beyond its South American neighbors. With lowered petroleum import costs in the following decade, and with Brazil's urgent press for more oil from its own pumps (rapidly reaching half of its consumption before 1985), there may be no need to convert the railroad to its intended electrification, especially considering the credit squeeze which has dimmed 1970s optimism.

Understandably, preliminary financial forecasts for CVRD's investments (and those of the government and foreign partners) were disappointingly overestimated, with iron, bauxite, and alumina exports coming on line nearly in pace with the timetable in late 1984–early 1985. With mining development and associated investments of $3.7 billion, the updated government plan of 1982, *Consolidação Plurianual de Prográmas do Govêrno 1982–85*, expected iron ore exports of 15 million tons annually (eventually up to 35 million), and about 750,000 tons of bauxite and alumina, to bring in about $630 million annually—a return of about 17 percent on investments. Had this been the early result, Brazil's trade and financial performance would have been measurably enhanced at a very crucial time, with the planned surplus of $2.3 billion (CPPG 1982–85, SEPLAN R.B., 1982). Brazil rose to seventh and sixth place, respectively, in steel and pig iron production by 1984, and to second rank (after the USSR, and shared with China) in iron ore. Thus, in terms of production and goal attainment, the plans laid in 1970 seemed accurate; however, state enterprises such as CVRD slipped badly on containment of costs and in reacting to indicated softness in the export marketplace.

It would be possible to end the CVRD-Carajás story on more upbeat terms by extending the performance accounting beyond the ending of the Figueiredo government's term in March, 1985. With such incredible accumulated resources to exploit, success could hardly be postponed beyond the early 1990s, when most of the other minerals—copper especially—would be being exported at full capacity. The fiscal restrictions and world recession of the late 1970s had such adverse consequences that the vast Matarazzo Group—Brazil's largest private enterprise in former years—and two or three of the iron-steel private or mixed corporations nearly collapsed. One, CIMETAL of São Paulo, did end up in the hands of receivers, and the Villares Group was only rescued by an upturn in the industry. Considering those circumstances, Brazil's heavy investments in basic industries such as steel furnaces and grand, "pharaonic" power and internal transport facilities were well justified. Even though world market conditions often undermined Brazil's ability to compete on a sustainable basis, especially after the OPEC petroleum cartel's success, without doubt the chosen strategy of heavy industrialization would have faltered without the extensive governmental investments it made during the 1970s and early 1980s in such infrastructure.

MAJOR BUILDING PROGRAMS AND THE EXPORT DRIVE

Once again, we find the remaining two policy instruments Moss cited, infrastructure and export incentives, closely linked, due to the influence of market conditions on Brazil's readiness to enter into competition with developed world products. Before the 1960s, Brazil was a market force in only three commodity areas: cocoa, sugar, and of course, coffee. With so many newly independent countries now eager to cut into Brazil's earnings and market share in those commodities, military leaders and technocrats foresaw severe limits to foreign exchange earnings unless they soon undertook investments in different exports promising a stronger price advantage.

As the leadership saw things, the best new opportunities lay *outside* the highly developed central triangle of Rio–São Paulo–Belo Horizonte. Critics, however, charged that behind that decision, political motives were responsible for introducing government investments in such unprecedented quantities into those states where congressional support was strongest, and where labor movements were either weak or altogether nonexistent. In fact, after futile opposition attempts to embarrass the government by an MDB Party–directed boycott of elections in 1974 had backfired, it became increasingly necessary for the PDS majority party leadership to apply its purse-string advantages judiciously, in order to hold a reduced margin of control in the hands of the supporting party.

The "Nation-building" Campaign

The Médici government intended, using an expensive National Integration Plan (PIN), to consolidate its strategy and thus try to popularize major programs for road and power dam building which had, in the case of the TransAmazon Highway at least, run into fairly extensive and vociferous opposition. The idea was that Brazil needed communication and energy facilities, especially in the outermost states, by which to induce migration and colonization of its vast, underexploited interior regions. Prior administrations had also preached "interiorization," with President Kubitschek's dramatic gesture in building Brasilia a prime example. Reluctantly, Carioca politicians and upper-level civil servants obeyed the order to transfer government offices to the new Federal District, but initially they conducted more of the government's business in Rio on weekends, or on the planes which shuttled them back and forth. Brilliant though it was in concept, the Brasilia plan still had not sold interiorization to Brazilians.

Another promising but insufficient scheme was declaration of Manaus, major river port in the heart of the Amazon, as a tax free port of entry. Tourism soon followed completion of an airport capable of landing new "jumbo" airliners at Manaus, as travel agencies abroad, as well as from within Brazil, began enticing tourists to view closeup this unique water wonderland, with its many broad tributaries winding through the tropical "green hell."

The initial concept of highway building in Amazônia included the continent-spanning TransAmazon Highway, a north-south transverse axis through the center of the interior northern states, and a perimetric northern arm. This would connect Brazil's major northern city, Boa Vista, with the unpopulated hinterlands on either side, running through the equally unpopulated interiors of Colombia, Venezuela, Guyana, and Surinam. Less than a fourth of the latter route, some twenty-five hundred miles long, was cleared but never paved, and eventually postponed. Relations with Venezuela in particular, and with the former Guianas states, had been frosty for many years. Some of the mistrust of Brazilian territorial hegemony was offset with the convening and signing of the Amazon Pact in July 1978 by each of Brazil's seven Amazonian region neighbors. The treaty in effect interrupted Brazil's plans for further development north of the main axis of the Amazon river.

Paving of the other Amazonian highway routes was interrupted or delayed for fiscal rather than political reasons, coming to an end only in 1986 with the completion of an extra, particularly viable leg, some nine hundred miles long, which connected Porto Velho in Rondónia to Cuiabá in Mato Grosso state. This was a region apt to appeal to the ranchers from Paraná and the southern states, who had proven more keen to migrate to the interior than the *Nordestino* migrants, who still headed toward Rio or São Paulo by the thousands every month. Cuiabá was also connected by the transverse axis route to Santarém, the second most important port of the Amazônian interior (after Manaus). The route of greatest complexity and length was, of course, BR–230: the Trans-Amazon Highway. This route, which ran from the edge of presently developed highways at Floriano (Maranhão state) to the Peruvian border adjacent to Acre (newly designated as a state), required 2,350 miles of storm-graded, all-weather highway crossing dozens of tributary rivers.

The proposed budget for the two transverse spans of the new highway was a mere $80 million (*Metas e Bases* 1970: 165), a figure that certainly strains belief. Plans for this huge construction program had been developing since the midpoint of the Castello Branco government, and there had been opposition to this outlay from the beginning. To scale down the cost figures, and thus to overcome opposition in the Congress, initial plans (not made public) were to only build high-grade gravel pavement and to have more than 100 bridges made of wood. As a consequence, to obtain funding approval—unlike the impression given in North American newspaper discussions of Brazilian "dictatorship"—the government so seriously underestimated costs and requisite construction standards that completion was deferred until the early 1980s, at a time when capital was increasingly dear. A true estimate, by the responsible official in charge of the National Department of Roads and Highways, was that the TransAmazon was costing about 500,000 cruzeiros (just over $100,000) per kilometer (Pereira 1971: 154), meaning that the net cost of the nearly 4,000-kilometer highways would be about $430 million. One reason for the deceptiveness was that the government was, in the 1970–1974 period alone, proposing to undertake construction of a vast network amounting to 82,000 kilometers of federal highways, allocating only 4 billion cruzeiros ($860 million). In essence, it was a "shell game" aimed at pleasing all regions.

Greater enthusiasm was generated by proposals to add to Brazil's electric energy generation, out of its untapped and fortuitously located hydroelectric potential. Some of it was to benefit the poverty-stricken Northeast, where the second longest of Brazil's rivers, São Francisco, couldn't compare in power potential to the tributaries of the Amazon, or to the Paraná on the border with Paraguay and Argentina. The centerpiece was to be the great Itaipu Dam, with minor cooperation from Paraguay, on the Paraná. Itaipu, with its cost-saving hollow chamber design reducing the concrete requirements by one-fourth, still cost $14 billion (of which Paraguay absorbed perhaps $2 billion). When completely on line, its eighteen turbines would have a generating capacity of 13 million kilowatts of power, making it the largest power dam in the world. Tucuruí, on the Tocantins River in Amazônia, also completed in 1984, and with a generating capacity of 8 million kilowatts, ranked fourth among the world's hydroelectric power dams.

It would greatly understate the scope of the plans laid in the years of military rule if only two hydroelectric projects were described. In the 1980 to 1985 period alone, nine further hydroelectric dams were added to the nation's power grid: two on the São Francisco, another (São Felix) on the Tocantins in Amazônia, and the remainder along the Paraná or its tributaries. One of the most remarkable projects was the Sobradinho Dam, in the driest part of the São Francisco River in Bahia state. Originally planned more for irrigation programs than for power generation, the cost, less than $100 million, had been too much for the government to finance in the Goulart years; and its 770-megawatt output (at high river stage) would not satisfy the local power corporation's anticipated needs. The regional power authority (CHESF) therefore opposed Sobradinho, wanting instead to build a conventional hydroelectric dam at Itaparica, nearer to existing public demand. The latter, costing more than three times what had been estimated for Sobradinho, required expensive work to relocate farms, dwellings, and small cities in its backwater, but it would produce 2,300 megawatts of power. That was much more than present public demand could absorb, meaning that it would have to pass on increased costs to its clients, unless the dam could be heavily subsidized by the government. More of the political ramifications of that policy issue are given in my earlier study (1973: 697–709) devoted to the politics of water resource decision-making in the Northeast.

The government's decision, lending to a better understanding of the way authorities resolved local issues of this type, was to build the Sobradinho Dam first, but to increase its headwater height to 43 feet, to slightly increase its hydroelectric capacity. This created a very shallow lake nearly 400 kilometers long with a reservoir capacity of 34 billion cubic meters. It also necessitated the rebuilding of five small rural towns inundated by its enormous backwater. For every compromise like this, there seemed to be an added price. In this arid climate where high rates of evaporation would be expected to reduce reservoir heights by 2 meters per year during drought periods, a shallow lake with a large surface area was far from ideal, especially for the power industry's use. The usual drought cycle was once or twice per decade in that region. Shortly after completion of Sobradinho, when Brazil suffered five consecutive years of drought in the Northeast, it became necessary to build the Itaparica Dam to augment power capacities urgently required to meet anticipated demand.

The Export Production Drive

Citibank senior economist Ronald Krieger (1971: 36), writing early in 1971 from a 1960s perspective, concluded that all Brazil needed to retain a favorable balance in its external trade over the next few years was a modest degree of diversification of exports and a steady market for its coffee. Fortunately, this was not how the leadership viewed prospects, for the global trading conditions, financing terms, and interest rates changed radically after 1973. Whereas coffee exports in the mid-sixties accounted for almost half of Brazil's foreign exchange earnings, a decade later the coffee exports were less than half of net external sales. By 1975 Brazil's imports exceeded exports by as much as $4.6 billion (1980 values), according to the InterAmerican Development Bank (IDB 1980: 403, 447).

Much of that deemphasis on coffee exports was intentional. There had been a well-planned and aggressively executed national program aimed at broad export diversification to produce rapid expansion of foreign sales. The companion effort, suppression of the rising import bill, had not been as well done, even if we disregard the sudden rise in imported petroleum costs. Eul-soo Pang (1985: 64), in his studies of the state enterprises, found that about 60 percent of Brazil's external debt was owed by state-operated industries. He concluded that it was their excessive purchases of new equipment, more than the crude oil purchases, which had extended the national indebtedness to the crisis stage. Adding to the problem was the fact that the six hundred or more state enterprises were running large deficits in the budgets, which had not yet anticipated net profits. Furthermore, he found that more than 70 percent of the outstanding loans had been incurred at prevailing commercial rates, negotiated at the London Interbank Offered Rate (LIBOR), whereas only 8 percent of the loans were drawn on the substantially lower U.S. prime rate. Of course, that rate was for preferred borrowers, but Brazil in the 1970s might easily have qualified. When petrodollars began flowing into European and U.S. lending institutions, they were only too happy to find clients such as Brazil seeking loans at market rates, who had stable governments and timely repayment records. The *estatais* unknowingly were made to look like chumps.

By 1970, agricultural exports accounted for only about 10 percent of net sales, while manufacturing contributed 27 percent. For the next fifteen years, agriculture's contributions remained fairly constant—fortunately helping at a critical juncture—while sales of manufactures gradually advanced to about 33 percent. Brazil's sales to the United States—more than twice that to any other nation—amounted to about 20 percent of net sales. Despite great distances (ideological as well as physical), Brazil now reached out to the USSR and to China, as well as to Near East customers (especially Iraq). Trade had been modest with former kinsmen in Angola and Nigeria, but those oil exporters became valuable trade outlets. When monetary obstacles arose, mutually advantageous barter terms were worked out, exchanging raw and semiprocessed agricultural products for petroleum. After cutting off military procurement from the United States, Brazilian factories were able within a few years to begin exports of arms, aircraft, and implements, thus responding to Iraq's war needs. Unequal trade with the USSR was similarly solved: turbine generators worth $600 million were needed for use in Ilha Grande Dam, on which construction began in 1982.

Trade efforts turned the corner from deficit to surplus in 1981, despite worldwide recession and the suddenly escalated costs of imported petroleum, but the net balance was still unfavorable because of the very high debt and service account payments Brazil was now making, at rapidly rising interest rates. Until 1983, the last resort for refinancing the debts—the International Monetary Fund—had not been approached. Instead, Brazilian borrowers and the government's bankers had fought the financial battles unaided. They felt some disdain, privately, toward various hemispheric debt victims who had recently knuckled under to the IMF's austerity demands that infringed upon national sovereignty. Brazil had even given symbolic assistance to Mexico with a loan when it teetered near default in 1982. But Brazil's turn came a year later. With oil prices and interest rates not yet descending, some lenders now balked at once again rolling over payment schedules. Each percentage rise in interest on existing loans was costing 600 million more scarce dollars in annual debt repayments, and when petroleum imports cost an additional dollar per barrel, the annual effect was to raise import charges by another $260 million.

Most if not all financial experts dismissed as impossible the proposal from Brazil's Central Bank president that, in 1983, a trade surplus of $6 billion would be realized through cutting its imports about 20 percent and boosting its exports nearly 10 percent. Actually, Brazil registered a surplus of $6.8 billion for 1983, with exports rising by over 15 percent. That performance was then exceeded—partially as the result of falling crude oil prices and interest rates—with a trade surplus of more than $13 billion, led by another 23 percent gain in Brazil's export sales (IDB 1986: 220). While this record was pleasing to lenders, the market gains which shifted to favor Brazil were earning it some overt animosity among rival producers and their governments. Signs of the politically slanted hostility that had grown up between Brazil and the United States in the late 1970s now threatened anew, as trade representatives seemed at times to have exchanged kid gloves for brass knuckles.

Initially, it was in agricultural commodities that intense competition grew between the two countries: sugar, soybeans, chicken, beef, and even orange concentrate (for which Brazil is now the number one exporter). Then competition developed in iron and steel products, some aluminum products, plastics, footwear, wood products and furniture, and finally, arms sales. Through barter—and by refusal to support Israel in the United Nations at such times as when the Arab-African bloc voted condemnations—Brazil took away from the United States a few food and raw material contracts. Retaliations followed, as the United States began to place tariffs on Brazilian steel products, footwear, and sugar, as well as graduating these and progressively more products from the GATT Generalized System of Preferences (GSP) duty-free list.

At times it was not the government but the autonomous state enterprises which provoked retaliations. An example was when, in 1983, the Tuberão steel mill—hungry for contracts with which to forge entry into the market as a newcomer—angered the British Steel Corporation's union leadership by undercutting British bids nearly 40 percent (seemingly below costs). Next year, the Tuberão marketers found a defunct steel plant (Fontana) near Los Angeles which could be resuscitated by taking 30 percent of its 2 million tons per year as raw material for further finishing, using new capital investments from CVRD, Kawasaki and Wilkinson. By such means, Brazil elbowed its way to a global marketing stature.

THE RESULTS AND THEIR SOCIAL CONSEQUENCES

Previous chapters sought to highlight areas of ideology and socio-political motives of the leadership from 1964 (and before) through the termination of military rule in March 1985. The following chapter will focus upon the willingness or the hesitance of the leadership to relinquish ruling authority, with an evaluation of degrees of success and failure on the part of the military elite to fulfill the mission they undertook. Having dealt so much with the guiding economic theories and applied policies, now it is time to consider the socioeconomic question of how policy choices affected the Brazilian people during those years.

It must be acknowledged that, while the economy of the country was thriving perhaps better than could have been expected through much of the twenty-one-year interval of military dominance over policy-making, the welfare of the majority of the people suffered. If one were to look only at broad socioeconomic indications, conditions when the military relinquished power in 1985 were not improved over what had been considered in 1964 to have produced the political crisis. The new indebtedness burden was only barely being repaid out of vastly improved production and arduously won gains in overseas markets. But where to go now? What new avenues were open, by which to regain a growth momentum that might produce another "rising tide" of national wealth, able to bring about the predicted elevation of incomes and welfare on the mass level that had not occurred over the past two decades? Higher margins of savings and investments—in economists' terms, greater ratios of increments of capital to output (ICOR)—would now apply, thus to hinder continued rates of economic development. Then, to the dismay and outcries of Brazilian government leaders, GATT and the World Bank began treating Brazil and a few other growing countries of the Third World, such as South Korea, less favorably, labeling them "newly industrialized countries."

Policies chosen by the military leadership from the outset adhered closely to the dictates of the Rostow thesis, which called for a big push toward the "takeoff stage," resulting in cuts in wage and welfare distributions so that the needed margins of capital investments could be taken from savings rather than borrowed. Of course, the end result of heavy capital outlays for high technology and equipment was heavy borrowing in addition to the enforced savings policy. Since this occurred at a time of liberalized credit and unusual expenditures for petroleum, circumstances have precluded a real testing of Rostow's theories. Dramatic growth has been achieved, but at an unconscionable cost to the welfare of the vast majority of Brazilians. Brazil's reward was to be reclassified as an industrialized country, no longer in need of preferential terms for development funding.

The borrowing became necessary because of the untimely, unprecedented exponential escalation of crude oil prices, which happened to be one of Brazil's most essential imports. The surge of profits from OPEC's oil sales were in turn responsible for two further adverse events: global recessions which came at the time when Brazil's export drive was likely to repay handsomely its borrowed investments, and then the sudden uptick of interest rates which drastically elevated the annual costs for debt service. We are left with excellent grounds for Brazilians to believe in leftist economists' direst charges about the injustices of the dependency syndrome, and with less than acceptable circumstances on which to weigh the validity of the Rostow thesis.

We could, of course, harshly judge the military elite for their willingness to test the takeoff thesis at some cost to the consumers and workers of their nation. If that judgment can also be suspended, because of the foregoing circumstances which led to an invalid test of costs versus ultimate benefits, there could be a better basis to evaluate Hirschman's theory about backward and forward linkages from the industrial sector to the agriculture and service sectors, through his "leading sector" predictions. Even if agricultural production and earnings flourished briefly during the brief time that Delfim Neto was minister of agriculture in the Figueiredo government, that growth was due to government subsidies and promotions rather than because of linkage demands generated through industrial growth. Likewise, growth in the service sector came about mainly as a government plan to give employment to hosts of seriously underqualified workers, not by responding to the forward linkage of the subsidized industrial sector. Naturally, definitive judgments such as these should have substantiation reaching beyond what could be derived from this study.

A major difficulty in rendering conclusive judgments about processes employed toward modernization and productive growth stems from the fact that so much of the changed economic conditions over the two decades came about not through the workings of free enterprise, on which Hirschman's thesis was based, but with what may be termed "forced draft" industrial growth, dominated by governmental regulation, planning, and capital investments. The agricultural sector, rather than being spurred toward modernization and productive growth, was made the servant of industrial expansion by providing cities with food and fiber at undervalued prices over which, predictably, they lacked alternate market opportunity. For example, in the political decision-making environment of the SUDENE governing council, presided over and under the control of nine state governors, it was only late in the period that there were many approvals given to agricultural development projects. That was consistent with the leading sector theory, which was only modified to treat agriculture more equitably in the 1980s, after Brazil found it had to actually import such basic foodstuffs as corn, wheat, rice, and those two staples of every Brazilian's diet: beans and beef. Investing in capital-intensive new industries was costing about five times what would have been required to provide equivalent levels of employment in agriculture. After the 1970s boom died, employment was no longer being created at a level needed to absorb annual increments of nearly a million new workers. It was clearly time for a policy change.

Inequities in the income structure—along with Peru, at the *worst* level in Latin America—did not improve and, judging from a special World Bank study (1984b), appear even to have worsened in the wake of the industrialization-export subsidization drive. The Social Integration Program (PIS) initiated by the Médici government had only a brief trial before fiscal imperatives effectively wrecked the voluntary parts which sought to address fairer wage distributions. The remainder of its requirements were only enforceable in the most profitable industries, mainly the best of the mineral industries and the multinationals, so that most Brazilians were left unaffected. However, the PIS program may have created important precedents, such as requiring salary contributions toward employment severance payments. These applied only after the employee had completed a probationary service (in most cases less than one year), but here again, the measure only affected salaried employees, not extending to the much more numerous hourly wage workers. Mandated fringe benefits of the PIS laws would add 75 percent to the base pay, not including such valuable government-funded benefits as comprehensive medical care, delivered under the Social Security and Welfare Payments System.

Even though twenty-one years seems remarkably long as a testing period for the ability of Brazil's military regimes to achieve measurable progress toward development goals, unusual circumstances have rendered the test inconclusive. Too much has depended upon worldwide changes and factors lying beyond Brazil's capacity to influence. The free enterprise system to which the government initially was committed, and upon which economic theories were based, was soon abandoned in the all-out drive toward what Rostow had predicted to be a self-sustained, autonomous stage of progress. At the period when Brazil enjoyed its greatest degree of economic success in the early 1970s, it seemed to its citizenry to have lost much of its independence, and the government tended to lose its legitimacy, as viewed from citizens' perspectives. This was thus perceived because the first leadership had so eagerly accepted droves of external—mainly U.S.—investors and economic advisers to help mount the drive toward what was to be national greatness and independence.

What about the relationship economically to the United States? The military regimes, starting with their export drive of the mid-seventies, assigned less importance to coffee as a strategic policy, and also less importance to the United States, as a pragmatic act. When I asked the EMFA minister (Armed Forces chief of staff), General Werner, whether he still considered the United States to be as important to Brazil's future as it had been in the past, he touched my hand to get my full attention, and said, "It is not as important as it was, but it is still *very* important to Brazil." From the emphasis and tone of voice, I sensed he had carefully pondered that question for sometime. His answer, given in the summer of 1984, typified the views of others.

Possessing ruling power, even for as much as two decades, does not compensate for long-standing developmental gaps, as efforts to build up the two weak regions—Northeast and Amazônia—demonstrate. Measured macroeconomically, the military regimes made remarkable progress, but the internal distribution may have worsened to such a point that the poorest were worse off than ever. The rich, as so often happens, only got wealthier, as the leadership should have anticipated from familiar economic process theories.

I am convinced that, in their choice of development strategy, the military leaders had anticipated shorter seasons of inequity and deprivation, and an end result which would have met with the broad approval of a majority: a self-sustainable, developed economic future in which everyone would be more secure. It is unfortunate, for analysis of development theories, that more was not achieved in the military rulership. The great misfortune of the petroleum price manipulation episode is that so many of the ever-resilient Brazilian lower class fared so badly.

6

Reopening the Political System under Cross Pressures

With each incoming president since 1964, including Castello Branco, earnest-sounding pledges of an early return to democratic processes had been uttered, and then seemingly forgotten. Indeed, for the first three presidencies, the end result of experiences with the cross pressures of dissident internal factions, and the multitude of economic and political challenges each had faced, was a sterner, less popular leadership group than there had been when each regime took office. Some of that downhill trek could be the inevitable consequence of having borne the country's many burdens unappreciated by citizens who could not know how little the leaders could do to make good on their promises. As previously discussed, the national development strategy adopted from 1964 onward held out little likelihood of an early benefit to most Brazilians' current levels of living. For many reasons, not least the perception that further delays in producing better incomes and living conditions might well be intolerable, by the mid-seventies the leadership showed real signs of seeking to end the military tenure of ruling power. But willingness to step down and return power to elected civilian leaders was not shared among those of the hard-line faction. They created most of the trouble that delayed attempts to reverse political autocracy.

One essential precondition to any reopening of "politics" to opposition from civilian leaders was to put down the guerrilla challenge; no authoritarian regime would allow itself defeat at the hands of its avowed enemies, least of all at the voting urns. President Médici's intelligence competence was a bonus in that he, as the recent head of Brazil's massive and effective SNI, may have inspired the confidence he needed to press reforms upon the reassembled Congress. He wasn't apt to be deluded into political overconfidence by the lopsided victory of the ARENA (pro-government) party in the 1970 elections, produced much more by the unwise decision of the MDB (opposition) party leaders to urge a boycott of that election than by public support of his regime. In any event, there was no inclination on his part to extend the move toward democracy further in the advent of the 1974 national elections, in view of the presence of strong political opposition and imminent prospects of economic recession.

LIMITED LIBERALIZATIONS IN THE GEISEL ADMINISTRATION

Since Geisel was a moderate military politician of the Castellist faction, one would expect to see early signals of planned redemocratization to come from his leadership. Three principal factors can be cited to explain why this pattern developed only late in Geisel's five-year term, even though he gave early promise of doing exactly this with his pledged "relaxation" policy *(distensão,* literally a releasing of tensions and governmental concentration). They were: first, ample evidence by 1974 that the Castellist line was very much in the minority; second, evidence that the preceding government had overstepped accepted limits of repressive policy-making in its efforts to counter the guerrilla menace to its own (not the public's) security; and third, the keen awareness of the near-stranglehold which the massive state intelligence-security network by then held on governmental prerogatives at every level. There may also have been a realization that the economic good times of recent years were nearing an end. Petroleum price increases on the nearly 300 million barrels Brazil imported in 1974 increased the country's external debt by more than 25 percent.

The military presidents, having no recognized popular mandate earned through democratic election, depended for their support in times of political upheavals upon two vital "pillars": the backing of the military elite (essentially, the army four-star generals collectively known as the High Command); and the inner circle of Brazil's capitalist core, i.e., the São Paulo–based financial and industrial magnates. The secret coalition-building arrangement within the military elite has already been explained, albeit in hypothetical form, in chapter 4. We have also seen how the São Paulo industrial-financial center dominated the fiscal and political "engine of progress" that elevated Brazil to newly industrialized status. More, however, can be learned about the role of the latter by a closer examination of the way that two incidents affected high politics within the Geisel administration.

São Paulo Hard-liners and the "Herzog Affair"

One could relate conservatism and even obstructionism toward proposed socioeconomic reform to the São Paulo landowners and financial-industrial elite who were close associates to army opponents of President Goulart in the 1960s, or if one wished, as far back as the 1932 abortive anti-Vargas revolt. The same type of political bias prevailed, centered again in São Paulo, during the 1970s. Again, the senior general heading the Second Army in São Paulo and the governor's military adjutant in charge of security for the city and state were like-minded stalwarts of the hard line. The president's chief "ambassador" to the São Paulo civilian elite was his minister of industry and commerce, Severo Gomes, who had a close relationship to the São Paulo governor and his friends.

To expert observers of Brazilian society such as Charles Wagley (1963: 72–79), wry commentator-visitors such as George Mikes (1961: 73–74), or epic novelists such as Errol Lincoln Uys (1986: 952–53), the *Paulistas* appear to be a distinctly different breed. Peter McDonough (1981: 83) saw the São Paulo elite as "the most insular of the regions" who very seldom emigrate and—though cosmopolitan by reason of their many ethnically diverse origins, including Asia as well as most of the European countries—"are extremely private, a collectivity with tribal qualities." The sum of those qualities, combined with a history of co-dominance of political power in the republican period up to the 1930s, and pivotal financial control in the era of this study, made for a unique setting from which hard-liners of the military elite could confront the president on crucial issues.

Despite the efforts of Geisel, and of his predecessor in the Planalto Palace in Brasilia, a shadowy volunteer organization in the São Paulo region known as OBAN (Operation Bandeirantes, here a seemingly patriotic reference to "flag-bearer" pioneers who extended Brazil's empire to its western limits) was prosecuting a campaign to stamp out any perceived antigovernment elements. In fact, OBAN in the mid–1970s was enjoying the open assistance of the Second Army's police investigative unit (part of the SNI security apparatus), the now infamous CODI-DOI. Brasilia, although aware that all was not right in the Second Army's security apparatus—which came not under federal but state control—apparently did not find it necessary to intervene until the Herzog case became a headline item.

As the Geisel administration had taken a body blow to its prestige in the November 1974 congressional elections, there was much more than normal interest in the comparatively smaller stakes of municipal elections scheduled for November 1976. Geisel was pressuring his ARENA party leadership to mount a comeback, in the well-founded belief that the local level—where patronage had always been a dominant factor—would remain its strongest base. However, the opposition, now emboldened, took up the challenge, courting the news media, which had also held grudges against the past authoritarian restrictions (now somewhat liberalized, but still advisedly limited to "good behavior" as sanctioned by the government). Thus the government found itself being assailed for mistakes, for the overly internationalist bias in its development policies, and for the unrelieved wage austerity which affected so many. The São Paulo and Rio de Janeiro urban centers became the favored battleground as of mid–1975.

Two events were especially worrisome to the paramilitary security-intelligence apparatus: Portugal's *military* revolution of 1974, because of ethnic ties, aroused fears of armed Bolshevism in Brazil's urban centers (far beyond what one might suppose to have been warranted); and an ugly incident of mob violence in Greater Rio de Janeiro had culminated in the wholesale sacking of government-owned railroad facilities. More enlightened consideration would have led to conclusions that Portuguese radicalism would not extend to Brazilians unless there was already a climate of near-revolutionary discontent; and even scant investigation would have shown that the pillaging of the Rio Centro Railways had grown out of intolerable overcrowding, hazards so serious that there were frequent deaths of riders commuting to low-paying jobs, and repetitive delays which were costing Rio commuters whole days' wages. At any rate, the climate for tragic misunderstanding, especially in São Paulo with its repression-minded military security force, was set.

Vladimir Herzog, as the news director for São Paulo's small educational television network *TV Cultura*, was among a corps of journalists critical of the government. He had previously been a journalist for the weekly newsmagazine *Visão* and for the frequently antigovernment daily, *Estado de São Paulo*, and had written items for the British Broadcasting Corporation in the same city. He was an experienced journalist who had weathered many seasons of self-censored journalistic employment, and he was Jewish. In a sudden, massive security sweep of more than two hundred dissidents (ten journalists and larger numbers of lawyers, professors, union leaders, and MDB party staff workers), Herzog was issued a summons to come in to the Second Army's security (CODI-DOI) staff center for questioning. His body was returned one day later to his widow in a sealed casket.

The "Herzog Affair" needed little impetus to arouse the passions of antigovernment activists, and even to the larger number of those who might previously have counted themselves as neutrals or even as government supporters. The brutality of the murderers was as nothing compared to their subsequent insensitivity in the coverup policy. The required investigation report included only an internal autopsy and perfunctory hearings at which no external representation had been allowed.

The public was then provided an obviously contrived "written confession" admitting that Herzog had belonged to the outlawed PCB (Brazilian Communist Party), and the official declaration that he had hanged himself in his cell.

This whitewash brought immediate recriminations not only from opposition figures but from the Catholic Church and the sizeable Jewish community in Greater São Paulo. Within a few weeks, the "big lie" became exposed when another journalist, also beaten during questioning and who had shared Herzog's cell, went before live television cameras to give the accurate version of how Herzog had died at the hands of his interrogators. Adding to the dramatic effect, the cellmate, Luis Costa—who had been released only two days after Herzog's death (evidently while panic reigned at CODI-DOI)—had been rendered unable to walk from his spinal injuries, and he had missing teeth and perforated eardrums (Flynn 1979: 496–97; *Latin America*, 1975: 346–48).

President Geisel, hemmed in somewhat by his army minister, Sylvio Frota, an opposition hard-liner under whom corrective action necessarily fell due, did not direct a thorough purging of the São Paulo Army establishment as he ought to have done. In a compromise dictated by the delicacy of his own mandate, he instead summoned the Second Army commander, Gen. Eduardo D'Avila, to a hastily convened conference, and obtained assurance that he would oversee immediate cleanup operations within the security division in São Paulo. D'Avila evidently did nothing until it was too late to save his own position. Another torture-murder, this time of a dissident metalworker named Manoel Fiel Filho, occurred in the same interrogation center only three months later, producing the belated purge and dismissal-retirement of General D'Avila.

The usually well-informed London newsletter, *Latin America* (1975: 302; and 1976: 14–15), substantiates the severe limits within which President Geisel was operating at the time. It seems that General D'Avila was a central figure in a planned coup d'etat, in which the other major figure was Antônio Delfim Neto then in "exile" as ambassador to France. Delfim's hopes to be the next governor of São Paulo had been thwarted by President Geisel while he was still only the military high command's nominee for the presidency. Delfim was then riding high as President Médici's finance minister, the most important and well-known cabinet figure. The conspirators had more than the usual need for caution because Geisel's protector in the First Army headquarters (Vila Militar) outside urban Rio de Janeiro, General Reinaldo de Mello, could probably have turned such a coup effort into a bloody civil war. Supposedly, the planned date for the coup was early December, soon after the municipal election results would become known. Though the police dragnet of opponents of the regime was seen as advancing the hard-liners' cause and support, especially in the São Paulo area, none of the plotters had counted on an inflammatory incident such as the Herzog affair; in any event, the plot was wisely dropped after public opinion soon afterward ran heavily against them.

One of the immediate consequences of the two deaths caused by torture in security interrogations at São Paulo was that the president determined to take firmer control over the whole military intelligence–police interrogation apparatus, beginning with a working group within the National Security Council, over which he and his SNI director were in control. Another outcome, of course, was the loss of prestige externally, as well as more intense internal political opposition to prolongation of the now unpopular military rule, already into its eleventh year. Brazil's "responsible pragmatism" in voting with Afro-Asian nations for the United Nations resolution branding Zionism as racism made for even greater alienation of the regime from its Jewish community.

The Politics of Succession and the Frota Affair

With sufficient recovery of personal standing on the part of President Geisel, at least with his own military vanguard, plans began to focus upon the naming of his successor, to be chosen in the final session of the present Congress. With campaigns between the ARENA and MDB parties contesting for victory in the direct elections of deputies and a third of the Senate in November 1978, the season was not lacking in political tensions. One important casualty, resulting from coming from the São Paulo conservative bloc (pressed in turn by industrialists and business leaders) was the hyperactive and rather unpopular minister of trade and industry, Severo Gomes. It seemed that Gomes had alienated the *Paulistas*, who then prevailed upon the president to call for his minister's resignation. Behind the scenes, Geisel had been tentatively working with Severo Gomes to attempt what, had it been successful, would have been a nifty finessing of the military hard-liner bloc, leading to approval of another moderate—Gen. Euler Bentes Monteiro (about whom more follows)—as the official ARENA and military nominee to become president. President Geisel had to cancel that ploy in order to retain his essential "second leg" centered in the São Paulo area.

Geisel and his chief strategist, retired General Golbery, had a draft amendment to the constitution ready for the assembled Congress to give its anticipated assent when it resumed in March 1977. The president expected that he would be able to assure election of his successor under the electoral college's indirect vote (in the past, more aptly termed a ratification of the High Command's selection) in a special session of the Congress. Constitutional amendments required approval by a two-thirds majority of each chamber, and with only a twenty-vote ARENA margin in the lower house (Chamber of Deputies) the amendment was defeated. Contrary to all that he had pledged two years before, and much chagrined at the solidarity displayed by MDB and dissident ARENA deputies, Geisel thereupon closed the Congress and by his emergency decree powers issued the amendment bill on his own authority.

This "April Package" had some revealing and very significant measures by which to attempt to assure a well-controlled election: (1) once again, the election of state governors would be indirect; (2) a third senator for each state would be elected by the state assembly (in most of which ARENA held majorities); (3) districting for the Federal Deputies (i.e., lower chamber) would be once more based upon the census data, rather than upon eligible electors, in effect adding to the strength of representation from the nonindustrialized states, where ARENA had always been stronger; (4) media restrictions on electoral advertisements (*Lei Falcao*), which had been decreed to the advantage of progovernment candidates in the 1976 municipal elections were now made permanent; (5) electoral colleges in each state were expanded to include some representation from municipal councils (in which ARENA had kept its majorities in 1976); (6) politicians deprived of their rights (ten-year sentences having by then expired) were permanently ineligible for elective office; (7) presidents' and vice presidents' terms in office were extended from five to six years; (8) the nomination date for president and vice president was brought forward from January 1979 to October 1978 (meaning that they were be elected by the current membership of national and state-local legislators); and finally, (9) further amendments of the constitution would be approved by a simple majority in Congress (reflecting the anticipation that the progovernment bloc would likely never again be capable of passing amendments by a two-thirds majority). As we shall see in the events to follow, after the 1982 congressional elections—in which the government lost control of the Chamber of Deputies—some of these measures calculated to retain control of the "election" process, had to be revoked.

While Geisel's heavy-handed dealing with Congress provoked some of his more democratic-minded colleagues, it regained for him the wavering support of the hard-line element and, it was supposed, his army minister, Gen. Sylvio Frota. Dismissal of D'Avila was acceptable to them, not only because his poor handling of the security apparatus in São Paulo had disgraced others in the army, but also because of his unseemly and openly political behavior. Lavish gifts and honors—some solicited, others received in feigned protest—had come to him from the *Paulista* industrial associations for whom he had done special favors. Yet, when handing d'Avila his dismissal Frota—in a quixotic gesture to appease D'Avila's civilian friends—issued an effusive congratulatory message to the general on his retirement.

It was understood, as in most democratic countries, that any cabinet minister served only at the pleasure of the president. Nevertheless the October 1965 "understanding" cited in earlier chapters, as a result of the so-called "White (bloodless) Coup" of the hard-line, required that the alternation of the president and army minister, always of the two opposed factions, would be kept intact as an assurance of good faith and peace within the elite. Geisel's first army minister, Gen. Dale Coutinho, had died in that office within the first year; and his replacement, General Frota, though of the hard-line bloc, had been initially loyal, if not altogether effective in that vital role as "ambassador" to his like-minded colleagues. As trouble developed in 1977, notably preceding the sacking of Minister Severo Gomes for his advocacy of an immediate reopening of normalized politics, it became clear to Geisel that Frota was cultivating his own candidacy as president. Geisel, meanwhile, had been working with Gomes behind the scenes to test the waters (among the army hierarchy particularly) as to the viability of putting forward a second moderate the aforementioned General Bentes Monteiro, to succeed himself. Sharp conflict with Frota was inevitable. Geisel considered Frota unacceptable; even when he decided, judiciously, to abandon the feelers regarding Bentes Monteiro (with Severo Gomes no longer around), he did not attempt an understanding with Frota. Instead, he began to groom his most obvious alternate choice and ultimate successor, Figueiredo, for whom he eventually had to wage a difficult fight.

Among other problems, President Geisel risked being upstaged and enduring "lame duck" status as a result of premature media attention and "presidenciable" contenders' efforts to promote themselves. By law, active campaigning should not have begun before May 1978, and by agreement within the High Command, consideration of whom they would nominate as next president was not to begin until January of that year. However, Frota, in the guise of service business, was already visiting even minor encampments far and wide—unlike any of his predecessors as army minister—and also courting leading members in the Congress. To match the excellent organizational network at the disposal of his rival, Figueiredo, who headed the cabinet-level National Information Service (SNI) with its security people at every level of national and state level government, Frota established within the army his own communication-intelligence facility, CIEX (Army Center for Information) complete with a Siemens Telex system that operated independently of the public telephone system in Brazil. However, whereas Figueiredo operated out of the Planalto Palace in daily contact with the president, Frota was not in such frequent association with the Geisel administration. On the other hand, General Frota was Figueiredo's senior and far better known and perhaps more popular with the army's other top-ranked generals. As a script for a first-class, disunifying service imbroglio, it was perfect.

By the latter half of 1977, Geisel's situation was nearly intolerable, because the legislative claque whose favor General Frota had cultivated began making speeches in their protected enclave, extolling the presidential virtues of the army minister, and inferring that Geisel was conspiring behind the scenes (which he was) to put together his choice of successor without the full consultation of the senior military elite as had been the accepted practice. It was later revealed that the president's Military Staff chief (*Casa Militar*) Gen. Hugo Abreu—liaison to the army, but also expected to be the President's most trusted confidant—was secretly backing Frota while preparing his own support base as the alternative choice.

The crisis and its rapid denouement developed on the weekend preceding October 12, which was a national holiday, when Geisel was no longer able to tolerate the meddling activities of some of the ARENA legislators and some retired generals who were taking up Frota's cause. He decided to replace Frota as army minister with his Third Army (southern region) commander, Fernando Belfort Bethlem, who conveniently happened to be on leave at the time, vacationing in Rio de Janeiro. Bethlem was a respected hard-liner with whom Geisel knew he could work; any other choice might well have been unacceptable to the High Command. Quietly summoning Bethlem to Brasilia for consultation on the eleventh, what *Latin America Political Report* (1977: 323) called "Geisel's Coup" took shape the next day (a holiday) when Frota was called out of bed to the Planalto Palace and asked to step down; upon refusing, he was told he was fired. Frota attempted to reverse the "coup" by calling an emergency meeting of the military High Command that same day, but before midafternoon the skirmish had ended with his defeat. Instead of assembling with Frota at the Brasilia Military Command's headquarters, nicknamed "Fort Apache," aides of the president met the incoming flights at the airport and guided each of them to the ceremonies at the Planalto, where General Bethlem was sworn in, and the luck of the winners toasted.

The "Frota Affair" did not end without some ill-contained acrimony, when he released a farewell letter warning his followers against the "imminent danger" they faced of being overcome in the "manacles of Marxist totalitarianism." It was unclear for a time whether Geisel's "coup" would sit well with his army colleagues, since nomination to be the army minister was one opportunity to which many aspired, and his choice normally would have been vetted within the High Command. As matters soon developed, Frota's cause was not taken up by any of his peers, and the instinct to rally around the president prevailed.

Passing the Succession to General Figueiredo

Having sidetracked General Frota, the nomination of João Figueiredo could no longer be kept out of the press and politicians' press interviews, even though Geisel attempted for awhile longer to give the impression that he was not yet committed to his choice. It was also important, considering that the official date for nomination was not yet at hand, to avoid further embarrassing the High Command, since it was indeed being left out. The media were not, however, easily deceived.

The excellent credentials and relatively neutral status of Figueiredo—vis-a-vis both hard-liners and moderates—were described in chapter 3. However, after the "rule" used to deny Albuquerque Lima consideration in 1969 because he was not yet at four-star rank, Geisel's nominee-to-be represented a new status problem. By moving the official nomination date ahead of October 1978 so that the present, safe ARENA majority could elect his successor, Geisel had fallen into an awkward trap: there would ordinarily be no consideration of Figueiredo for a fourth star until November 1979. With some unusual personnel shifts, fine-pencilled calculations, and authorization to promote an extra general (due to having an army general serving as SNI director, a cabinet post), it was possible by an extra promotion session to boost Figueiredo to the top rank in April 1978, denying promotion in the process to some deserving seniors who were, as a consequence, forced to retire. Among those not promoted was Hugo Abreu, who had served Geisel as Military Staff chief in the Planalto Palace; this also caused considerable stir.

Meanwhile, the MDB leadership had been giving serious thought to nominating the ex-senator (presently Minas Gerais governor) José Magalhães Pinto; but turned then to General Bentes Monteiro. Before accepting the MDB nomination, the general carefully ascertained through SNI and media (deniable) channels that his rumored stand in the opposition slate would not produce untoward recrimination. The MDB party leadership likewise tested the military elite's reaction to a civilian candidate before reaching the conclusion that their best odds of averting a military intervention lay in the direction of putting up a rival general as their nominee. The relatively strong showing of Figueiredo and his civilian vice presidential running mate, Aureliano Chaves (Minas Gerais governor), over General Bentes Monteiro and his civilian running mate, Magalhães Pinto, was probably abetted by the fact that Magalhães Pinto was a defector from ARENA, and the pattern of dissension which the two MDB candidates displayed during the election campaign. As we have also seen, the deck had been unfairly stacked against the opposition through the decreed "April Package" of amendments to the constitution's election rules.

Before turning over the reins to his successor, President Geisel was determined to see through some of his promised aims to liberalize and decentralize authoritarian Brazil. Even though it was to occur when economic problems loomed large, his actions were real favors to Figueiredo, in that the hard-line bloc couldn't be as obstructionist during what remained of his mandate as they might when the newly elected leader began his six-year term in office. With but five more months to go, after having assured Figueiredo's victory when he guaranteed the ARENA nomination as well as the composition of the Electoral College by his April 1977 package, the president decreed two fairly dramatic steps toward reopening politics: the abolition of the sweeping powers of the president under the hated Institutional Act #5, and the reinstitution of habeas corpus laws.

THE FIGUEIREDO GOVERNMENT AND THE *ABERTURA* PLAN

Well before the inauguration date, the Brazilian press corps was buzzing with behind-the-scenes leaks and abundant speculation about what the new administration would bring. Apart from the usual huddling over designations as cabinet ministers, most of the interest centered upon discussions between Geisel, Figueiredo and the behind-scenes strategist for both, General Golbery, about ending the artificial and increasingly obsolete two-party system. With electoral slates prominently identifying by *sublegendas* (historical ideologic caucus groups) notable leaders of different factions in each of the ARENA and MDB rosters, it was clear that a multiparty system represented the true tendencies of politicians, and perhaps most of their supporting voter blocs.

It was revealed early in the discussions that Figueiredo believed that five parties would be the ideal, and that Golbery saw three as most preferable. Both believed that the very attractiveness of membership in the one progovernment party—for patronage, power, and perhaps effective leadership roles—would be sufficient to hold together most of the present membership of the current ARENA roster in the legislative bodies. Realistically, it seemed evident even then that the liberalization of the party structure was primarily motivated by the eroding capacity of the progovernment party in the last half of the 1970s to assure the government of congressional approval of its measures. The plan could easily be assessed to be a plot to "divide and rule." It also tended to reveal some overconfidence and political naivete. Discussions began over how to deal with the problems of the opposition politicians upon returning to Brazil from exile, and of what might be done with the numerous enemies then in prisons.

The First Year's Bold Reopening Measures

President Figueiredo might have been forgiven had he delayed the initiation of plans for *Abertura,* considering the labor-related problems he had to deal with almost as soon as he was inaugurated. For the first time in the fifteen-year military rule, whole industries such as automobile manufacturing and metallurgies were out on unsanctioned strikes lasting through much of April and May 1979. In Brazil, not only under the authoritarian period but for many years prior to 1964, the organization of labor was top-directed rather than through the workers' democratic efforts. One of the consequences was that strikes first had to be voted upon and then authorized by the government before they were "legal." Since the strike actions, centered in São Paulo state, had not been given governmental approval, some right-wing politicians and hard-line regulars felt that immediate seizures were called for, notwithstanding the probability of violent resistance and bloodshed. However, the administration chose to wait out the strike actions at some cost to the national economy, believing the end result would be less rather than greater labor unrest. Also there was a coincidental plan to improve working-class wage policies in any event, just as soon as Congress would approve.

Within the first nine months, using the existing, narrow plurality which the ARENA party afforded him in the Chamber, the new president obtained passage of a general amnesty bill forgiving thousands for political offenses, while retaining control of judicial prerogatives over the fewer numbers whose crimes had included use of violence or the accusation of murder. Even before this, by decree powers, hundreds—possibly thousands —of those charged with purely political offenses (ordinarily defined as charges lodged under the Law of National Security) had been released; this was not clouded by subterfuge, for the result was in fact to empty prisons of all but convicted felons. The last to be freed were the politicians, in what was an almost totally new atmosphere for half of the Brazilians under twenty years of age. By law near the end of 1979 they too were allowed to form and join political parties according to a new organic concept.

The reorganization of the reconvening Chamber of Deputies and Senate in March, 1980 produced a reduction of the government's supporting bloc from 5 percent (the margin ARENA squeaked out in the November 1978 elections to the lower chamber), to a mere *1* percent in the newly organized Democratic Socialist Party (PDS). In fact, there would have been no majority at all if the leaders of the PDS had not been able to coopt a splinter of the largest opposition party, the Brazilian Democratic Movement Party (PMDB) by the president's choosing its spokesman, Ibi Ackel, to become justice minister. Of course, with the "bionic" third (indirectly chosen) senators strengthening the PDS bloc in the upper chamber, total control of the Congress was not at risk; however, there were many times when the government might be stymied if it could not produce a majority for its programs in each chamber. It was one thing to say that the opposition, now divided into four party organizations, would be equally incapable of unified initiatives. In their opposition role, it was often enough to bring about compromises favorable to strong minority blocs if the PDS leadership was aware that it had insufficient votes to pass its legislative bills.

Though the future seemed formidably unpredictable, it seems fair to say that, in a strong first year's showing, Figueiredo had won widespread admiration for his regime's determination and parliamentary skills, so that in many cases he now had Congress and affiliated constituencies willing and probably able to help him as the administration entered its second year.

Preparations for the "Open" 1982 Elections

By arguing that holding of municipal elections, scheduled for November of 1980, allowed too little organization time in many of Brazil's rural areas, Figueiredo obtained the assent of Congress to postpone the election of mayors and councilmen until two years later, simply extending the terms of incumbents until early 1983. This pleased those who were relieved of the labors of a campaign for two years, redounding to the benefit of the PDS party. The natural consequence for the politicians of the country, however, was to create a package of elections for every government level except the presidency, which was occupied until 1985. Most of all, appetites were whetted by prospects for the first time since 1965, of electing governors for half of the states, including most of the major ones.

Though the government party had profited in various ways by the *Abertura* policy, carefully administered to preserve strength in as many instances as possible, there was one overriding liability: economic contractions worldwide were producing for Brazil some unresolved, severe fiscal and social problems. Inflation had returned with such force that the government, not ready to renounce its "crawling peg" minidevaluations at monthly intervals (or oftener, if that had not been too burdensome), had the discretion to rename the policy the "trotting peg." Cost-of-living wage increases, as in prior regimes, lagged badly.

Samuel Huntington (1984: 213), citing Spain and Brazil as noteworthy examples of the past decade, pointed out some of the great challenges reform-minded leaders face, "having to maneuver skillfully between the stand-patters opposed to any democratization on the one hand, and the committed dissident and opposition groups demanding immediate dissolution of the authoritarian state, on the other." It is essential, he pointed out, that the leader appears to be in control, not acting under duress, in that process. Such was the situation with President Figueredo, when he was disabled in September by a heart attack, eventually treated by a coronary bypass operation done in Cleveland, Ohio, with several weeks of forced inactivity lasting into November 1981. While he might have reaped useful sympathy and support at the time, he was hardly seen as being "in control." To the credit of the leaders and the opposition, the civilian vice president Aureliano Chaves was permitted to govern effectively in that critical period when Congress was debating some controversial changes to the constitution which would once again tend to favor the PDS party in the critical national elections the following November.

When the seriously worried military and civilian leadership returned to calculating electoral odds in March 1982, having narrowly gained passage of the measures proposed in the preceding congressional session, further changes seemed necessary. Another "April package" was thereupon presented and narrowly adopted. Recognizing that the 1977 change allowing amendments to the constitution by simple majority votes posed a likelihood of reversal of what had been recently adopted, now they moved to slam the door by once again requiring passage of changes by a two-thirds majority. Further steps designed to hold the PDS bloc's narrow advantage following the 1982 elections included the prohibition of ballot splitting between parties, and requiring all political parties to submit a full slate of candidates in every precinct. If one saw ticket splitting as a corruption of democratic processes, these two measures would appear mutually consistent and fair—but the smaller parties were being heavily disadvantaged. Many had strong constituencies in only certain areas; now, if they wanted to contest the election of the most attractive offices, such as governorships, they were forced to deplete their coffers and human resources in the rural areas where such parties had little or no followings. Also, adding to the so-called *Lei Falcao*, there were now prohibitions against mass media uses on behalf of announced candidates prior to the official opening of electoral campaigns, as well as prohibition of campaign advertising during the final four weeks preceding the election. Incumbent politicians, naturally, could not be thus "silenced" when and if they were to use the media otherwise, as for instance for speech-making at a ceremonial occasion. Again, the president and PDS were favored.

Despite whatever perception there was of an unfair set of rules of the game, politicians and their numerous active supporters entered enthusiastically into campaigning at the allowed season, producing tons of folios and literature, and a surfeit of shrill public debate. Minor parties such as the heavily urban labor parties, of which there were three (Labor Party, Brazilian Labor Party, and Democratic Labor Party) worked hard despite the odds. The idea of an open contest at last, even if not yet fair to all, appealed strongly to the exuberant and competitive Brazilians.

It may have been the best of all possible worlds for the president and his majority party that the November 1982 outcome could justifiably be claimed as a victory for various factions. The Brazilian Democratic Movement Party (PMDB), which had tried to be a broad opposition front to the military government by virtual obliteration of its ideologic policies and perspectives was a winner in nine of the state governorships—many of greatest real significance—and placed 200 deputies (out of 479 seats) in the lower chamber of Congress. There were sizable gains for the PMDB. On the other hand, the progovernment PDS bloc placed 234 deputies in the Chamber of Deputies, and kept its sizable majority in the Senate, aided by the third, "bionic" Senate seat system. While it had won twelve state governorships (a thirteenth was a PDS governor not required to run at that time), they were not the most important states. Most significantly, however, now the PDS party had for the first time less than a majority in one chamber of the Congress. "Winning" was very much a matter of personal states of mind.

Now that no party had a majority, worried deputies and party leaders on either side of the aisle in the Chamber of Deputies saw the necessity for some conciliatory move, simply to avert repetitive stalemates in attempts to enact bills presented to the Congress. By the time Congress convened in March 1983, a temporary resolution was achieved by the brief marriage of the leadership of the PDS party bloc to the thirteen-member contingent elected from the PTB (Brazilian Labor Party) headed by Ivete Vargas, whose uncle was the founder and hero of the party, Getúlio Vargas. This provided sufficient support to permit the reorganization of the lower house by electing the president and other leaders.

The Challenges That Were to Follow

With Brazil's turn inevitably following Mexico's brush with default on its debt payments in 1982, Figueredo government leaders necessarily pared the budget wherever possible, and reluctantly chose to present the Congress with bleak policy alternatives. Those could be readily reduced to two: *default,* or acceptance of several austerity measures that were being dictated to the country by the International Monetary Fund. Worst of all, both the leadership and its supporting politicians in Congress felt constrained to openly commit themselves to a policy of cutting the wage adjustments to only 80 percent of the rising inflation rate. Understandably, the cumulative effect stemming from past wage injustices was a dam ready to burst. The regime, by now deprived of laws which had formerly protected the ruling authorities, obviously felt threatened.

During the next period of legislative sessions, the president had to depart for Cleveland to have additional heart surgery, again leaving his vice president as the acting head of government and state affairs. There was a perceptible difference by this time, however. Despite the six-year term—or possibly as a result of having lengthened the waiting time for those harboring presidential ambitions—now not only Chaves but also one or two of the cabinet ministers and an ex-ARENA governor of São Paulo (now one of the PDS deputies in the lower house) were beginning to prepare their contests for the government party's presidential nomination. *Abertura* had been so thoroughly implanted that it was now widely assumed by the media and the public that the next president would be a civilian. Thus, a military president with health problems, but with more than two years yet to serve, was being prematurely reduced to "has-been" status, in the midst of what now loomed as Brazil's darkest hour, based on most views of the economic prospects. While the denouement of this debt resolution crisis is left to the concluding chapter, it seems fitting here to point out that the sudden, sharp drop in petroleum import prices worldwide—along with moderated IMF-demands concerning measures imposed to close the annual budgetary deficits—did wonders in restoring manageability to President Figueiredo's fiscal difficulties.

Regarding a personal choice for successor, Figueiredo wisely withheld any intimation of his choice, for good reasons quite apart from the diminution of his own authority which doing so would have produced. He showed somewhat less support for Vice President Chaves's candidacy, despite their amicable relationship and the graceful way that Chaves had fulfilled his responsibilities on two occasions without seemingly seeking to usurp more of the office's glamour and self-enhancing potential than others in that position might have done. Retired army Colonel Mario Andreazza, now his minister of the interior, but also a veteran cabinet member in each of the previous three administrations, seemed to be the "anointed" candidate of the military elite, and speculatively also of the president. However, Andreazza was exploiting the wealth of opportunities of his post to build up a formidable bank of political debts from every governor and even mayors of every sizable town in the country. It was reported that the interior minister, over a three-year period, had personally visited every one of Brazil's nearly four thousand *municípios*, making some type of governmental presentation to always grateful and flattered minor politicians.

Ex-governor Paulo Maluf, a third presidential aspirant, was also busily traveling to all parts of the vast country, testing his support and recruiting backers for the upcoming party's nominating convention. Maluf, of Lebanese descent and one of the wealthiest millionaires in Brazil, had a sizeable following from his governorship of São Paulo (always a valuable career launching pad) as well as among the conservative Northeast bloc, since he had become a federal deputy operating from the Congress in Brasilia. He had astutely foreseen that the Chamber of Deputies would be the key arena for brokering the next transition of the presidency, and it was also the kind of place where his technique of political payoffs worked well.

Figueiredo recognized that having three strong candidates to choose from would almost inevitably divide the PDS party, yet there was little he could do except withhold his endorsement for as long as he could. Whether it was a tactic (to help him remain silent) or accurate, unscotched rumors floated for awhile that Figueiredo was open to the possibility of a further constitutional amendment to extend his term by two years. Though he was probably the most popular of the five military presidents, this maneuver did not gather many supporters. For both parties and the Brazilian people in general, as the second decade under military governments drew to a close, the inexorable attractions of electoral combat took over.

For obvious reasons, the PMDB opposition in Congress could not realistically have expected to be able to overturn the odds to impose their wishes for an electoral amendment—direct elections for the presidency—with the required two-thirds majority. Even so, beginning in March 1983, Federal Deputy Dante de Oliveira's proposed such an amendment which gathered enormous support subsequent months. The *Diretas já* movement represented a vivid demonstration of Brazilians' strong wish for a voice in choosing the next president instead of merely watching while a remote Electoral College (Congress plus some selected state assemblymen) cast its vote. Passage of an amendment was not impossible, in fact, as had been proven within the current Congress twice in the past year. With enough crossover PDS dissidents, both Chambers had overturned Figueiredo's Decree Law acceding to the IMF-directed 80 percent rate for automatic wage adjustments, rather than 100 percent of inflation as in the past. They had also been able to restore the previous automatic allocations from federal revenues for basic education and for sharing tax revenues with states and *municípios*. When the issue was sufficiently publicized and widely seen as just and popular, there might be enough PDS "rebels" willing to risk their future legislative careers.

The *Diretas* (direct elections) movement eventually caused the most multitudinous outpouring of public interest in Brazil's history, reaching its peak in major cities a week or two before the scheduled Chamber vote on April 25, 1984. Masses of half a million gathered festively but peacefully in Rio and, by unofficial estimate, as many as a million thronged downtown São Paulo to demonstrate for democracy at the grass-roots level. To no one's great surprise, the amendment failed in the Chamber, twenty-two votes short of the needed two-thirds majority, and therefore never came to a vote in the Senate, where a defeat may have been inevitable, even if extremely awkward for the government.

The increasingly assertive opposition next tried to knock down the Law of National Security, which had particularly thwarted journalists by its clause covering "offenses to public authority." Anticipating a clash that would do no one much good, officials of Figueredo's inner council offered their own revision to move that clause and additional offenses from military to civil jurisdiction. It was a palatable compromise, reducing the "crimes against national security" from about forty per year to half that number. Even so, it left untouched the stern prohibitions, triable as before by a military court, against defaming the president or heads of the legislative and judiciary bodies.

The liberalizing track record of President Figueiredo's plan of political Opening, *Abertura*, had made him an outcast by 1984 among the hard-line element, particularly among those operating from powerful positions in his former intelligence apparatus, the SNI. They had equally committed obstructionist colleagues within the army's Center for Information (CIEX) and the police interrogation and terrorist detective posts, the infamous CODI-DOI centers. Though they did not by any means operate with a majority of collegial support within the military elite as a whole, as chapters 3 and 4 have substantiated, the threat they posed to completion of the transition to civilian rule had to be taken seriously. Obstruction could produce chaos and severe disunity if not success, ultimately confounding the president's intended reopening. Whereas President Geisel had courted hard-line support, now President Figueiredo counted heavily upon public support for his *Abertura* to keep the intelligence staff at bay, while he pressed forward with its promises. He was helped in this regard early in his term by public reactions to two instances of repressive excesses, amounting to crimes for which they were found responsible.

The first incident was the "Rio Centro" bombing on May 1, 1981, which misfired in what had apparently been a plan to break up a leftist concert and rally in the heavily populated theater district, and would have cost many lives if it had succeeded. When a bomb exploded prematurely in a car driven by a CODI lieutenant, wounding himself and killing a CODI sergeant, the mandatory army inquiry attempted a whitewash. By 1981, the press was much freer to pry into the case which the public had recognized as an attempt by the hard-line to terrorize anti-government elements. In due time, the sordid details came out publicly, thanks to the investigative work of Belisa Ribeiro (1982), a staff reporter of Rio's largest newspaper, *O Globo*. Even then, the obstinacy of army authorities managed to keep the case "closed," provoking the heated objections of navy and air force judges on the Supreme Military Court (STM), which had the duty to approve the army report.

The image of the intelligence community dipped even lower following the death of Alexandre von Baumgarten, a prominent progovernment journalist who had edited the newsweekly *O Cruzeiro* until it folded. His death by a bullet to the head was initially covered up as a "boating accident" when his partly decomposed body had washed up on a suburban Rio beach. However, evidently fearing assassination by the SNI, on whose payroll he had been during the *Cruzeiro* days, Baumgarten had planted a highly detailed and incriminating dossier in the hands of the staff of *Veja*, Brazil's largest newsweekly, to be published in event of his death. It particularly implicated General Newton Cruz, deputy director of the SNI (who was subsequently tried but not convicted for Baumgarten's murder and other crimes), along with other members of the intelligence service, in various criminal activities. He let it be known that he had been recruited by the SNI to revive *O Cruzeiro* as an outlet for planted news and editorials favorable to the regime and the SNI and specifically critical of the *Abertura* policies. Funding had been withdrawn on assessment that the *Cruzeiro* journalism was having little effect on the public, after which publication soon ended. Baumgarten had also disclosed that SNI funds had been used to win the contract for clearance of wooded areas of the Tucuruí Dam backwater—which had also been badly mishandled—for a promised lucrative investment by CAPEMI, the capital investment management firm for the military retirement funds. That contract was eventually rescinded for noncompliance, proving to be an albatross around the necks of lower-level agents, but probably gaining many thousands of dollars for the promoters. Among the intelligence community's "neutralizations" detailed by Baumgarten, the most sensational was of the SNI's murder of engineer Souza Faffe, an employee of the Rio de Janeiro Telephone Company. He had evidently been engaged by the SNI in bugging operations for the intelligence service, and had then tried to shake down some of his military colleagues (as perhaps Baumgarten was also doing) with the illegal information he had obtained. Finally, he had prophesied that his killer would be General Newton Cruz.

According to *Latin America Regional Reports* (RB 83–04: 3), Baumgarten managed to further torment his persecutors from his grave, in his posthumously published novel, "Yellow Cake." In it, Baumgarten related (as "fiction") astounding details of high-level corruption, including the covert sale to Iraq of 70 tons of fissionable uranium oxide ("yellow cake") usable for reprocessing as bomb material, with the huge profits going to Paulo Maluf, who was then São Paulo governor. Though he used a fictitious name for Maluf, there was no mistaking his identity in the novel, which also detailed a multimillion-cruzeiro bogus loan and interest payments scheme for handsome profits, which the same São Paulo governor used to selectively reward political allies—military as well as civilian—through manipulation of accounts created falsely in the state bank of São Paulo. Both of these sordid tales were widely repeated by the media throughout the country, just as Maluf was making his bid for the presidency. Maluf was the favorite of the SNI and the service faction it represented, not only because their conservative beliefs coincided but because Maluf was already clear on his stance that there would be no revanchist inquiries about police or terrorist abuses by the military over past years. With trials or inquiries preliminary to trials of top members of Argentina's military governments prominently reported in Brazilian newspapers, not only Newton Cruz but most of his fellow workers in the intelligence community were strong backers of Maluf.

It had been assumed, ever since votes for the federal and state legislatures had been counted in November 1982, that the election of the PDS nominee by the already chosen Electoral College was a virtual certainty. The rules set up by recent amendments prohibited legislators from defecting to the opposite parties on key issues, such as the upcoming election. Nevertheless, as early "nose counts" for the PDS nomination began to show Maluf as the likely winner, party members of moderate (i.e., reformist) leanings began to look for an alternative to the Maluf juggernaut. Political huddles of likely dissident PDS legislators, seeing moderate Tancredo Neves as the probable nominee of the opposition, looked for an escape. Many of the military elite were among them.

Military Reservations Concerning Restored Democracy

During two research visits to Brazil, preceding the 1982 elections for all but the presidency and in 1984 preceding the two major parties' nominating conventions, I inquired about what seemed to be the two leading questions confronting the military elite, as the nation struggled toward political "normalization." Too much can not be claimed for that survey per se, especially since so few agreed even to respond on such sensitive matters (not for attribution, and with few exceptions not recorded mechanically nor by apparent pencil activity). Numbering in all only twenty-four respondents—of which all but four were then on active duty and all but two above the rank equivalent of colonel, almost half were from Rio de Janeiro, none (other than by informal and incomplete questioning) from São Paulo, and only a few were from Brasilia, Recife, Belem, and Porto Alegre—there was the further difficulty that all but eight were interviewed in the 1982 period, rather than at what became a more critical season in 1984. The results, therefore, have some importance, but they are not necessarily representative.

The first question asked was whether they considered Brazil *ready* then for a return to democratic participation. The second, asked in deliberately veiled terms, sought to determine whether the respondents felt the military elite *supported* the *Abertura* program. The actual question was whether *Abertura* was then succeeding, and what if anything would be necessary to complete the program's aims. Those whose answer to the second question seemed to foresee serious obstacles to *Abertura's* successful conclusion were arbitrarily counted as if they harbored negative attitudes. With that caveat, the fact that nearly three-fourths of the sample appeared to be actively supporting *Abertura* seems somewhat surprising. On the first "readiness for democracy" question, the evidence was mixed and more controversial. Nearly every respondent listed numerous aspects of Brazil's situation that frankly worried the military, and it became basically a subjective matter as to how they were to be categorized in "yes/no" fashion. In 1982, nearly half judged Brazil ready for redemocratization, yet several clearly felt that security would too quickly erode. A small majority expressed the belief that it would be best to wait for awhile. By 1984, seven out of eight unequivocally responded that it was time to give democracy an unrestricted trial, and the one less committed to the yes-no answer seemed to feel that another delay might be quite tolerable, even though he was unsure of how to arrange such a plan. Overall, I count the question as essentially unanswered, in that a bare 54 percent actually seemed to believe the country was really ready to be governed peacefully by a civilian leadership. For my part, the responses were credible insights by well-informed and responsible individuals who fully appreciated—far better than their predecessors had in the 1960s—the depth and range of the challenges and difficulties of governing Brazil in the 1980s.

Alfred Stepan (1988: 59) cited two major concessions that President Figueiredo and his High Command colleagues required, as a priori agreements in return for their approval for any civilian politician as next president: the firm guarantee, supplementing the 1979 general amnesty law (then as in 1984 seen as reciprocally binding on civil and military accused of some criminal action), of no revanchist accusation against the armed forces leaders such as the Alfonsin government was then doing in Argentina; and continued support for the military elite's most favored state enterprises—the arms-ships-aircraft industries, and the fledgling "informatics" (computer hardware-software) industry, which was still under debate in the Congress amid heavy lobbying from the United States. In both cases, the government sought to control radical impulses from within the present congressional opposition by tying together its minimum demand, reciprocal amnesty, with its most nationalistic legacy—durable protection for Brazil's infant but vital computer-related industry. Debate on the latter divided the opposition sufficiently to allow passage of the mini/microcomputer protection bill in October 1984, temporarily assuring protection of some twenty thousand jobs in that industry, but also dimming prospects for joint-producer agreements with U.S. and other foreign giants of the computer field, at the consequent risk of sliding Brazil backward into obsolescence. The side effect was also to deal the Maluf candidacy a blow, in that it was well known that he intended to abolish the *reserva de mercado* bill and to throw doors open wider to foreign technologic investors.

During this period, the near-assurance that Maluf had locked up the PDS nomination brought together a sizable defecting splinter of the PDS legislators in collusion with Vice President Chaves and leading politicians of the PMDB parliamentary blocs in urgent eleventh-hour consultations. What had loomed as only conceivable, given the rules that punished party defections and the acknowledged capability of the pro-government members of the Electoral College to elect the president's successor *if* they held together, became a reality in the week preceding the mid-August nominating conventions. The so-called "Liberal Front" of the PDS, estimated to number more than the necessary margin when added to the PMDB votes, made amply clear that they intended to hand the victory to the opposition. To lend the appearance of legality to that action, they named their splinter the Liberal Front Party (PFL), and after caucussing with PMDB leaders, the opposition "wedding" was named the Popular Democratic Alliance, and later simply the Democratic Alliance. The legality of the defection and new coalition did not seem to bother various party leaders, who very soon busied themselves courting potential strays in the Electoral College and counting votes.

Conclusion: Election of Neves-Sarney Ticket

During his final year as president Figueiredo, as had his predecessor, continued to play his cards close to the chest, not consulting his top army colleagues. His course was difficult, to be sure, but by provoking distrust and ultimately disinterest, he lost most of the influence which routinely belonged to the office of president. He did, in due time, decide that Tancredo Neves would not only be the nominee of the opposition but the probable winner, and privately held close consultations over the aforementioned vital prerequisites for his (and the armed forces') support: assurances of no revanchist trials, and preservation of the fledgling armaments and informatics industries, on which the military leaders were counting to forge an assured modernization and future strength. With those assurances being readily given all sides breathed easier, and the politically active headed for nominating conventions in August, while the remainder followed their countrymen on the customary vacations. Predictably, Neves and Maluf won their respective nominations in what for Neves was essentially an acclamation vote. To tie together the two parties, and incidentally to carve into Maluf's strength among northeastern legislators, the vice presidential nomination went uncontestedly to the former PDS congressional party leader, José Sarney, who with Vice President Aureliano Chaves had led the PFL defection in protest to Maluf's political tactics. The vice presidency was generally viewed as an ornamental slot, even though Chaves had twice governed as acting president during the extended incapacitations of Figueiredo. Even though Neves was an elderly man, at age 74 his health and capacity for stress seemed adequate; as a politician, Sarney was well known and admired, but it is doubtful that many of the Democratic Alliance gave thought to his capacity to lead the country through its most challenging future years.

As Stepan (1988: 57–58) discerned, and as my abbreviated survey had indicated to me, the mood of the military elite was a bit mixed. Essentially, they were resigned to the transition to a civilian presidency, but they held reservations about how well that process might turn out. Some civilians, such as Delfim Neto and Ernane Galvêas who had been in positions of extreme influence as ministers of planning and finance, respectively, were out in front of military contemporaries in opposing a civilianization of political leadership at that time. Rumors, significant enough to become formal charges, were circulating about private, profitable deals each of them—and some unnamed military collaborators—had made over recent years. Delfim's military attache during his ambassadorship in Paris alluded to a lurid dossier which could have led to very damaging charges against him. Combined with the intelligence community hard-liners, Figueiredo's embarrassments came at a time when his own enrichment, nepotism, and allegations of his son's illegal activities further limited his ability to lead.

The indirect nature of the presidential election made for a dull style of campaigning by each party. The business of obtaining commitments from members of the Electoral College was of a back-room nature, rather than of publicly seeking public support, perhaps undermining what was supposed to be party discipline favoring Maluf. He and his prominent civilian running mate, José Magalhães Pinto, did more clashing than agreeing on the occasions when either went to public debates or press interviews. Little by little, the PDS party seemed to fall apart at the seams, beleaguered as they were by having to defend the current administration's record while also promising reforms and improvements. Tancredo Neves's stock began to look so strong that he concentrated on solving transitional affairs, even lining up prospective cabinet associates. Neves met privately with each of the three service ministers, assuring them of his solidarity with their most urgent demands. In the case of Army Minister Walter Pires, Neves even offered to appoint him to the cabinet as welfare minister (which he accepted).

As the January 1985 Electoral Congress vote drew nearer, the Neves bandwagon became more apparent. After General Newton Cruz—ever true to the hard-line camp—announced his intention to set his Brasilia forces on full alert to preserve order during the voting process, the army minister at last acted to halt what could have been seen as a threat to the legislators themselves. Cruz was abruptly transferred to a post beneath his rank, as second in seniority in the army's personnel department. With that move, rumors of a desparate coup attempt by the hard-line evaporated.

The actual voting for president became a tepid affair, with the Neves-Sarney ticket drawing 480 votes to the Maluf-Pinto's 180. Immediately thereafter, President-elect Neves spent most of his three-month transition period in exhausting consultations with members of each party and the bureaucracy. Then, armed with the necessary grim facts to formulate his planned assault on the bankers of the world, Neves launched into a globe-girdling expedition in pursuit of assistance to bring Brazil's lagging economy up to speed, and to restore its debt-ridden coffers to normalcy. His moves were chronicled daily in the media, while Figueiredo's stature diminished daily. It was not widely known that Neves was nursing severe ulcer problems which, on the eve before he was to take the oath, March 15, became so painful that he had to undergo immediate surgery. Tragically, he may not have had the most expert surgeons at Brasilia; and he never recuperated. In his place on the appointed day, José Sarney accepted the sash of the presidency as acting president. Brazil had a civilian in the presidency at last, but without much joy. Anxieties turned to deepest mourning five weeks later, April 21, 1985, when Neves died and Sarney became Brazil's unanticipated president, due by the existing constitution to rule until March 1991!

In the concluding chapter, while offering a summation of the findings from this study of a lengthy military ruler, and my conclusions as to the capacity of such regimes to undertake the challenges of national development, we shall also look at the economic and political legacies which the military elite left in the aftermath of their "mission in mufti."

7

The Results and the Legacy of Military Rule

In the preceding chapters and in the introduction, more questions have been raised than an investigation of the present scope could undertake to answer. With that realization, I am consoled by the thought that it might destroy much of the charm of studying the "Brazilian style of politics" if there were no remaining unexplained mysteries. In this final chapter, quite a few major points which have been illuminated to various degrees by this study are restated here, in summation, as part of my conclusions.

In view of the frequent mention by international news and editorial media, it may not need to be noted that, for the vast majority of Brazilians today, life now is no better—in fact, by many criteria worse—than that which existed in the pre–1964 days. To whatever degree deserved, a likely consequence of the twenty-one years of authoritarian rule has been to adversely alter the general public's image of the military services as a collective institution. And yet, due no doubt to worsening standards of living under severe economic stress, one finds the first civilian government in equal or greater disfavor. As noted in the print media (Riding 1988: E1, and 1989: 12; *Latin America Regional Reports, Brazil* RB 87–08: 3), especially among middle-class people, a certain nostalgia lingers today for the more prosperous and orderly, "better days" under President Figueiredo and his four military predecessors.

Without doubt, the political life of Brazil as a republic for the past one hundred years has been dominated by the presence of a military elite ever threatening to overrule or intervene by force in the most important political issues of the country, virtually all of which assertedly affected their concerns for "order and progress." Until 1964, interventions had been of brief duration and had enjoyed the support of the politically influential civilian elite. As noted in chapter 2, this acceptance by the public of military dominance or significant influence in politics had been confirmed in the past by frequently nominating and even electing to the presidency (especially since 1945) senior military elites. We can do little more than speculate about the acceptance of future efforts on the part of armed forces officers or the whole institution to exert political influence. Available evidence such as "unofficial" surveys just after installation of the Sarney government reported by a London-based Latin America newsletter (*Latin American Regional Reports, Brazil* RB 85–09, 7), and a few interviews with senior military officers by myself and by Alfred Stepan (1988: 57–59, 64–67) strongly suggests that the feeling within the military elite has been that the movement toward civilian empowerment and military reprofessionalization is not only acceptable but inevitable. Even so, doubts were expressed anonymously over the future stability and integrity of politics under civil leadership. Those fears have not been allayed by unfolding events.

Before this book appears in print, Brazilians will have elected a successor to the indirectly elected Sarney regime, scheduled to assume the presidency in March 1990 in what promises to be a watershed event equal to the compromise 1988 Constitution. This concluding chapter is devoted to a retrospective review of the lengthy military interlude, which bids to overshadow political affairs for at least another decade. With as many as thirty separately chartered political parties—however unviable many now appear to be—potentially entering into tentative political alliances to elect the next president, it may only be the new practice of a runoff balloting of the top two vote-getters a month after the first national elections that can rescue Brazil from the weaknesses that led ultimately to the massive intervention of 1964. No matter how well this process works in bringing to power a president capable of unifying the nation and mobilizing its vast resources, much can be gained from a review of the successes, failures, and persistent political obstacles bequeathed by the military leadership.

SUMMATION OF FINDINGS FROM THE STUDY

Warren Hoge (1983: E3) observed, in what was the lowest year of the Figueiredo regime, that seizure of power in Latin American countries is far easier than the subsequent exercising of political ruling power. Though the retention of those powers in their own hands for an indefinite time was a marked departure from past practice, Brazil's military leaders have always been far more "political," in the civil-military continuum, than North American or European model institutions which, in so many other ways, they chose to emulate. This viewpoint is shared, and more fully elaborated, by such long-time observers of Brazilian militarism as Frank McCann (1979: 506–7), Thomas Skidmore (1988: 262–73), Alfred Stepan (1988: 103–4, 123–27), and Jordan Young (1972). Whether the nation is thus fated to remain politically immature for years to come is not clear to Brazilians or their friends. As so often happens, even dedicated "scientists" are readily led toward favored outcomes by their personally held norms. It is with that recognition that this study was directed, as its first research effort, toward scrutiny of the factors which unified most of the politically active military elites in the decision to remove President Goulart from the *Palacio do Planalto*. The prerequisite of institutional unity and the evident importance of political views held by different factions within the elite led to concentrated attention on the ideologic factor in several different contexts.

The Ideology-Unity Nexus

The events and the motivations of the military leadership which led to Goulart's removal and the Coup of 1964 have been ably and fully discussed in such works as those of Skidmore (1967) and Stepan (1978a). While I do not differ with their conclusions, in this study I emphasized the comparatively close agreement existing within the three armed services, as well as across common generational (i.e., rank group) lines in 1963, based upon my own essay literature analysis on three variables: attitudes toward development policy, internal security roles, and international relationships. That study, extended by five-year intervals through the period of military rule, and another which focused on the major fount of military ideology—Escola Superior de Guerra (ESG)—formed the basis for several significant conclusions concerning the ways and means the military elite used to find their way through minefields of factionalism and economic stress.

Anticommunism. The Cuban revolution and aftermath clearly swayed and to some degree polarized the military elite in the early 1960s. Four years after sweeping out Castroite elements and pro-Goulart officers, concerns over internal security peaked when several guerrilla movements rose up against the regime, concentrating this time not in the Northeast and planned rural focos but in the major cities. That threat was effectively ended by 1972, after which my survey revealed a steady decline of concern, even within the army, over internal security policy. Nevertheless, the issue of prevention of communist penetration remained alive, even while hard-line anticommunists within the services (centered within the "intelligence community") witnessed legalization of both communist parties (pro-Moscow PCB, and Maoist PC do B), and the installation of leading ex-communists in major elective offices such as the governor of Rio de Janeiro (Leonel Brizola) and present mayor of

São Paulo (Luiza Erundina de Souza). While the cadre of viscerally anticommunist conservatives within the military elite has declined, latent intolerance toward even leftist populists who have tended to make common cause with, or otherwise cater to, Marxists and Castroite revolutionaries are very much present if relatively silent today. A movement similar to that which planned the move to oust President Goulart would not be hard to revive if, for example, Leonel Brizola were to occupy the presidency (as polls continue in the late 1980s to suggest), and then to exercise some of the same haste and misjudgment of Goulart in seeking a leftist base for far-reaching structural reforms.

Attitudes Toward the United States. The mistake of the first government under Marshal Castello Branco was to fall out of touch with the industrial elite and the public in general, while opening Brazil up to an influx of capitalist enterprise from abroad, much of which came from the United States. It was a mistake in that the leadership did not enjoy the sympathy of the public—not originally for ideologic differences so much as for almost ignoring traditions of consultation, dialogue with other elites, or even public relations. Overfriendliness with American military advisors and businessmen led to open contempt for alleged *entreguistas* ("deliverers" to foreign exploiters), and feelings of envy mixed with alarm over the possibility of losing Brazilian nationalist ways and values. Those feelings turned to outright antipathy in specific quarters, and a broad turn by the late 1970s, from pro-Westernism toward a protective nationalism. That change was spurred by clumsy actions on the part of the U.S. administration to curtail Brazilian ambitions to develop its nuclear power (and potential for bomb-making?), and to act upon its newly declared policy of leadership in the human rights area. The end, at least for the foreseeable future, of the "unwritten alliance" between the United States and Brazil, despite a return to respectful goodwill and vestiges of personal friendships that will endure in any case, was also predictable for economic reasons. Comparable size and dominance within respective continents does not bind the nations together sufficiently to offset the effects of the stiff competition for markets which has developed lately in such worldwide commodities and products as iron, steel, food and fibers, consumer goods, electronics, and military armaments. The onerous burden of debt repayment, most of which is owed to North American banks or to global lending institutions such as the IMF and World Bank (where the U.S. influence is usually judged to be dominant) further aggravated the relationship. The "legacy" of a staggering debt burden—largest in the Third World—receives more discussion below. At this point, it suffices to add that Brazil's maturing, capitalist economic system under military stewardship has altered, apparently irrevocably, the former era of almost unquestioned filialty of earlier Brazilian governments.

Economic Development Policy. Opinion and government policy turned from a posture of openly attracting and welcoming foreign business investment in the first decade of military rule to one of economic nationalism and trade protectionism. In this matter, it should be added that, in similar fashion, comparable protectionism was being imposed by the industrialized world as well, in reaction to early 1980s global recession, and recognition that each country was now experiencing increasing balance-of-trade problems from Asian and European competitors. Moreover, there was the growing phenomenon of automation and capital-intensification encroaching upon the ability of states to provide gainful employment to its entering youth, despite the new era of family planning and the "baby bust."

Although there was division for awhile over the respective merits of "internationalizing" Brazil's industrial drive, through openness to foreign investment, versus continuation of protectionism and an inherited—and politically popular—import substitution policy, the military elite was in general agreement with the government's decision to concentrate investments in the industrial sector, and as a consequence to impose austere wage and subsidy policies on agriculture and the government-services sectors. Difficulties arose in sustaining growth and debt service payments, amidst recession and stiffening competition in the global marketplace. Agreement about the austere wage policy began to crumble among officers equally squeezed by inflation, especially when defense of the policy became fruitless over so many years, with no betterment in sight. Increasingly, absence of a spirit of optimism robbed the government policymakers—such as Delfim Neto, who maintained till the end of military rule that denial policies would win out—of lower ranks' support. It was another illustration of the adage, "Success has many fathers; failure is an orphan."

Centralization in the State. Early confidence, based most of all upon the on-the-shelf studies at the ESG of virtually all of Brazil's many intractable development problems, and the ability of the military regime—freed indefinitely from inhibiting effects of election politics—to conquer each obstacle it faced, did not long endure. Yet, with the added prodding of external investors and development aid institutions, including for a time specific requirements under the U.S. Alliance for Progress program, state intervention in the economy, massive rituals of centralized plan publication, and creation of hundreds of state corporations institutionalized under the military governments. My survey of the professional essay literature revealed virtually no ideologic foundation for the imposition of socialism per se. It therefore seems clear that decision centers over the past two decades regarded government control of the economy, to the extent being practiced then, as remaining faithful to the capitalism model under circumstances requiring extensive state nurture and protective direction. Since so much of the economic policy-making was by civilian technocrats, rather than under military control, this discontinuity of ideologic belief and practice was allowable for pragmatic reasons. Typically, the military elites directly concerned were much more goal-oriented than ideologic in their approach to policy-making and administration.

One additional factor lent itself to this "statization": ensconced in the more isolated and concentrated environment of Brasilia, rather than in the easygoing and more cosmopolitan bureaus of Rio de Janeiro as in former years, inbreeding was more likely.

Conclusions About Military Ideology. Most of the twenty-one-year period has been chronicled by national and overseas media and academic observers as a struggle for power between so-called "moderates" (Castellistas) and "hard-liners" (Costistas). In my research, while not denying the foregoing premise, several findings merit reiteration:

1. For the period immediately preceding the 1964 crisis and throughout the final decade of military rule, the above two groups were apparently outnumbered *among the politically active elite* by a less vociferous "democratic nationalist" faction, which was not particularly opposed to the influential role being played by the United States in Brazilian affairs, but was not willing to see that influence grow appreciably. This group, variously labeled by other observers in the 1960s era a "legalist" or "barracks" group, was more firmly committed to nonintervention in political affairs committed to nonintervention in political affairs by the armed forces, wanting instead to draw a clean line between such matters and the professional concerns of the services.
2. Interservice rivalries, though occasionally front-paged, as in the issue of whether naval or air force pilots would operate from the aircraft carrier *Minas Gerais*, never seriously threatened the unified support of the three services for their leadership.
3. Durable and understandable (even typical) attitudinal cleavages between officers of the colonel–naval captain rank group and their general-admiral-brigadier seniors showed up with regularity in the survey of professional literature, even though these differences of ideology also did not threaten breaches of unity. Supporting the familiar expectation that ideologic attitudes will not change much upon attaining maturity, I also found consistencies of viewpoint on issues such as internal security policy and the nationalist-internationalist dichotomy enduring over time. Thus, lower-ranked essayists' viewpoints, aggregated in an empirically sound manner, varied in similar fashion from the mean scores five and ten years later, when they and their career peers would have progressed to the colonel-captain ranks, and to the top ranks. In similar manner, the colonels' group showed similar viewpoints—often at variance from the seniors group—when they would likely have advanced to the general-admiral-brigadier echelon five or ten years later. To repeat, the differences were not unity-threatening.

4. In a familiar (to Brazilians) but nonetheless internationally unique way, the two power-contending factions (i.e., moderates and hard-liners) with presidential aspirants found a way to peaceably resolve the "spoils of victory" problem in what I labeled an "alternation agreement," following a coup-threatening conflict in 1965. As detailed in chapter 4, the presidency was chosen by the top-ranked High Command of the three services, was rotated successively between the two factions, and was kept secure by imposing in the post as army minister ("watchdog") a senior general of the opposite faction. My hypothesis about an alternation agreement has no confirmation by principals in past processes, but it is borne out with admirable consistency through classification of major role-players. Certainly the behavior exhibited is typically Brazilian, i.e., to avert violent conflict through compromise.
5. The Escola Superior de Guerra still enjoys prestige and excellent high-level support, but it no longer plays a large role in shaping national development policy. ESG policy papers developed from study groups or staff collaborations tend to go on the shelf at the ministries, and even more go no further than the Armed Forces General Staff (EMFA) headquarters in Brasilia.

Industrialization Drive Policy

Objectivity is somewhat difficult to maintain in attempting to assess the achievements of the military regimes in carrying out the intended push to self-sustained progress as an industrialized nation. It is clear that the effort was successful to some degree, as one sees in the 1980s reclassification of Brazil as one of the few states recognized by the World Bank as a "newly industrialized nation." The chief difficulty with resting the case on that fact is the realization that, as any right-minded observer must acknowledge, there is so much underdevelopment and poverty in Brazil that regions such as the Northeast could be compared to Bangladesh. If one then reflects upon the accompanying fact that a deferment of more equitable wealth distribution—in fact, acceptance of even worse income inequity—was an intentional policy of the third and fourth military governments (those in charge when economic fortunes might have permitted redistribution policies), little credit for policy achievement can be granted.

I may encounter much criticism for having extended myself in chapter 5 to defend the decision to limit income distribution, in the 1960s and early 1970s, as better policy than the available alternatives: to encourage internal consumption through income enhancement (i.e., to spend oneself toward development, which I find illogical), or to borrow as liberally as possible, in hopes of enjoying more favorable terms of repayment later on. Brazil did the latter, while denying income to its working-class majority, but circumstances encountered after 1974 left little alternative, in view of the massive infrastructural building programs which the government had begun (and could now ill affordable to suspend) prior to the unique OPEC-instigated petroleum price escalation, which spelled financial disaster for Brazil in particular. Though, according to public declarations, the last two military presidents had wanted to improve the levels of living of the poverty-stricken masses, there was little either could attempt beyond palliative half-measures. Putting such justifications aside, let us consider how much was accomplished by the military governments in the industrialization drive, and what the costs may have been to the whole population.

Economic Growth. As described in chapter 5, there were two periods, 1968 to 1973 and 1983 through 1985, in which the Gross Domestic Product attained remarkably high growth rates, in each time exceeding all or nearly all other Third World states. Intervening periods of recession are explainable by reference to external factors in the global marketplace—OPEC's price escalations and monetary or financial retrenchments in the developed world—and by what may be assessed as the cyclic workings of macroeconomics. We cannot adequately judge what might have been the performance of the national economy under a nonauthoritarian regime, and I am unwilling to attribute major responsibility for the comparative success of the era to an absence of competitive politics or to superior leadership. The results speak for themselves with mixed verdicts.

Using data from the InterAmerican Development Bank (1986), which summarizes in 1984 valorized dollar amounts what was reported in 1985, the GDP grew from $75 billion to $250 billion—233 percent—over the twenty-one years, during which the population grew by no more than 67 percent. Per capita incomes—however inequitably they were distributed, as will be treated next—grew from $850 to $1900 over the same interval (IDB 1986: 389–94).

Consistently with the declared economic growth strategy, the value of manufactures advanced by 230 percent over the two decades, as compared to 100 percent growth in agriculture, and 200 percent for the tertiary (government-services) sector. As an inevitable, and not necessarily advantageous, consequence of the chosen development strategy, urbanization grew from about 50 percent in the mid–1960s to 75 percent by the mid–1980s. Even though the creation of the National Housing Bank and other social improvement measures attempted to meet that growth with answers, such as the planned relocation of substandard urban squatters to sponsored apartment blocks, the growth of *favelas* surrounding Rio de Janeiro and Guanabara Bay, and in every other major city in equal or greater measure, gives the strong impression of no improvement overall, and in fact probable retrogression.

Income Maldistribution. It makes a great deal of difference, as I hope to clarify with illustrations, how one treats the types of economic activity and compensation experienced by the lowest deciles of a population in a less developed nation such as Brazil. Many if not most of those unfortunates are often unemployed or underemployed. Children at very young ages are working full time without pay in family enterprises. Unreported income is an endemic "given" in such economies, not only to avoid tax payment, but because it is often illegal, and certainly unregulated. With monetary valuations changing daily in worst cases, it may be judged that an equal or greater level of gainful work is dealt with on a barter basis. The same applies to trade in goods as it does in the services sector. Even so, comparisons by the same processes (i.e., by the same statisticians) provide useful comparisons.

An illustration of the confusion about income distribution can even be found in studies from the same source—the World Bank, in this case—using what may well be the best data available. In table 25 of its World Development Report (1984a), which in Brazil's case was based upon 1972 information, the bottom quintile received a shockingly low 2.0 percent of the total national income, and the next quintile was little better off with 5.0 percent. As Stepan (1988: 123–24) pointed out, this figure would mark Brazil as the worst (most maldistributed) case in the democratic world. In the very same year, the World Bank's more focused country study (1984b: 130) promulgated data attributed to the Brazilian Central Bank (Carlos Langoni, contributor) based upon 1980 estimates of the income distribution; the lowest two quintiles were a bit better off with 9.7 percent of the national income, and the top *decile* gained 47.9 percent. This compares rather closely with the 50.6 percent reported (for 1972) in the World Development Report (1984a).

In a special report internally distributed as a "working paper" and summarized with commentary by Brazilian economist Paulo Singer, as commissioned by Latin America Newsletters (*Latin America Regional Reports, Brazil* RB 80–04, 6–7), Guy Pfefferman and Richard Webb of the World Bank argue that others' reports of deterioration in equality of income distribution may be exaggerated, because of the great margins for error I have also cited. Even so, they and Mr. Singer agreed that levels of inequality had no doubt increased. The point of disagreement is that Pfefferman and Webb carefully distanced themselves from the sharpest critics by pointing out that absolute incomes had improved for all Brazilians, at which point Singer seems to waffle, and I withhold further judgment.

The Political Legacy and the Future Challenges

One may point with factual accuracy to two or three quantifiable measures of the two decades under authoritarian political rule, and judge rather harshly what has been the military legacy to the Brazilian people. Inflation, except for the few months of relief when the 1986 *Plano Cruzado* was initiated, has soared into triple digits (possibly beyond, briefly), gravely imperiling daily life for the laboring and middle-class consumers. Overambitious investment programs and well-founded allegations of high-level corruption have led to the Third World's highest external debt burden, estimated by 1985 to be just above $100 billion by the Inter-American Development Bank (IDB, 1985: 210). To those two "misery indices" one could add the figures for unemployment, which are inaccurate but averaged upwards of 20 percent in the 1980s. By any standard of measure, life in Brazil is grim, and appears to have worsened steadily in the 1980s, with the democratization of politics having failed to improve the circumstances, to say the least. The same picture has applied, equally if not more, to all but one or two Latin American countries with lengthier current governments one could call democratic. For that matter, outside of the Pacific Rim, Third World economies worldwide have been devastated by the same events which inflicted misery upon Brazil.

Since it seems inconclusive that military authoritarianism caused or directly contributed to the foregoing adverse results, other than indebtedness—about which more follows below—let us turn to other aspects of the political legacy for which more direct responsibility may be attached to the five military governments. Here I refer to the norms and political image they bequeathed.

Public Political Participation. Having denied its citizens direct, meaningful exercise of the vote for two decades (by my count, 1965 was the date of interruption, not 1960 as some have reasoned), it would be logical to suppose that a majority (realistically, all Brazilians under the age of forty) would have become disinterested, or at least unacquainted with political activism. The converse has been the case, concluded from the very intense, broad levels of preelection campaigning and audience attentiveness produced in the first "open" elections for all but the presidency in 1982, as well as for the runup to the congressional-constituent assembly voting in the fall of 1986. Further evidence is available from the intensity of activist behavior, even though from the outset it appeared to be an exercise in futility, during the 1984 *Diretas já* campaign for open election of Figueiredo's successor as president. At that time, peaceable but far from passive masses jammed city avenues in every state at festival-like rallies energetically pressing the Congress to amend the constitution, to give them the vote. Rio's half-million and São Paulo's million (according to semiofficial estimates) *diretas* supporters cared mightily!

How could this enthusiasm have been sustained? In this study, or for that matter in any other I have encountered, no foundation has been laid from which to answer such a difficult question. What can be contributed toward an explanation is the likelihood that, over the entire period, *leadership behavior* was acceptable to the extent that relatively few potentially "concerned" citizens lost faith in the exercise of political choice at elections. Opposition was curtailed, but not so severely squelched that *diretas* advocates had no ready-made followings. Political life was far from "dead." Among aspects of approved political behavior, substantial credit should be granted to the regularity of important power-transition processes, absence of any *caudillo*-type power broker system, use of extensive civilian expertise in executive positions, preservation of judicial restraint over the executive through the Supreme Federal Tribunal (even at those times when Congress was suspended), and the voluntary decision, starting in 1978, with suspension of sweeping emergency decree powers, to reopen the political system.

Reforms of the Political System. The aversion of leading military figures—many of whom personally waded in the political pond—to pre-1964 "politics" had focused upon how meaningless "fronts" of power-brokers with little in common had turned elections into elite-level divisions of the spoils of victory. The remedy was to abolish essentially personalist parties, replacing them with the ARENA-MDB two-party system. Though soon fragmented, and in time dismissed as an unnatural importation and therefore a failure—as an exercise in reinforcing the presidential system which is so dear to the military leadership—it may ultimately presage a similar type of reform. One needs only to recall the public reaction to the 1961–1962 parliamentary experiment, which they rejected by a five-to-one margin in the January 1963 referendum, to harbor some doubts about the level of public support the Congressional bloc enjoyed in the 1987–1988 period when they seemed on the verge of again installing a parliamentary form of government. Perhaps the astute provision of a presidential runoff between the top two candidates in the 1989 presidential elections will prove capable of restoring rationality and a modicum of stability and support for the next regime, in spite of the thirty or more active parties.

The Debt Problem. The most troublesome legacy for the Sarney government, and for its successors for the remainder of the century in all probability, is the massive external debt amounting by the end of the 1980s to $110 billion or more. Until 1983, while at the depth of a national (as well as international) recession, Brazil held off its creditors with a vigorous, subsidized export drive which produced trade surpluses of as much as $12 billion. It was enough to preserve a limited hard currency reserve and keep payment accounts current without resort to IMF conditionality-based bridging loans, but at an enormous cost in terms of capital lost to the national economy, and to payment of decent wages to workers. Since the transition to civilian rule, policymakers have vacillated between reluctant accession to international lenders and IMF terms, the Cruzado era "shock treatment," and, in 1987, to a brief moratorium on payments to commercial bank lenders. Each effort has met with little or no success. "Debt-for-equity" and proposed "debt-for-nature" swapping has only slightly reduced levels of external debt, as have the Baker and Brady proposals put forth by the United States in efforts to induce repayment performance.

Brazil was probably the most inviting prospect in the late 1970s for lending out what Geoffrey Smith (1983: 73) aptly termed the "sudden flood of petrodollars pouring into an already enormous Eurodollar overhang," more than two-thirds of which was handled by the commercial banking systems. As Smith assessed the problem, bankers had made two crucial mistakes: offering much shorter-term loans than usual, and placing them at attractive, variable rates, to protect what were viewed as loosely-secured, under-investigated borrowing proposals. It was a credit opportunity Latin Americans had long sought but never before experienced. Clearly it was an era tailored for error on the part of both lenders and borrowers. None of the parties involved could have anticipated the vigor and consequences, in terms of interest rates, with which the United States (in particular) attacked its inflation problem by sharply increasing the prime rate, thereby catapulting most trading nations into recession and sharply depressing commodity prices.

Like its relatively decentralized federal governing system, Brazil's foreign debt was diffused in ways that had led to looser control than that of some of its neighbors. Of the total debt of $100 billion as of early 1985, only $22.5 billion was a direct responsibility of the federal government. Another $14 billion had been incurred by the Central Bank, mainly out of defaults that had been guaranteed to various lenders. The Central Bank also had transitional responsibility for about $5 billion due to its role in the monetary exchange processes in linkage with Brazilian commercial banks. Various state and municipal governments were accountable for debts in the net amount of $4.7 billion. The remaining $54 billion of indebtedness was the specific responsibility of the more than 450 state corporations, each which had enjoyed autonomous capacity to borrow funds, and which were for the most part losing money daily.

In view of the above, belated efforts to sell off the most serious losers among the state enterprises was one of the most obvious measures taken to regain control over the financial disaster. Since the late 1970s, state corporations had to submit borrowing proposals for screening to a secretariat within the Ministry of Finance charged with controlling their spending habits. Other means of control included the Economic Development Council (CDE) and the National Monetary Council (CMN), and the government's representation on the governing boards of each corporation, whose initial charter and in most cases chief executive officer depended upon high government authority for authorization and appointment to power.

The debt problem, by its overwhelming size, has posed not only the issue of gaining control at the top—subsequently centralized in a new state holding company under the Finance Ministry, AGEBRAS—but of hewing to an acceptable repayment policy. So divisive is this aspect, in a country nearly overcome in holding together its popular support in the face of impoverishment, that national policy has wavered between nonpayment and submission to external demands. No less than four (to date) changes have taken place in the office of Minister of Finance during the Sarney administration. Aside from whittling away the quantity of the debt through debt-equity swaps and such means, the obvious recourse—which could only be undertaken after internal opposers to repayment and impatient creditor banks abroad had witnessed the sharp limitations for either side in any unilateral moratorium—was to reschedule variable-rate, short-term loans. Negotiations between February 1987 (moratorium date) and November 1988 ultimately led to the acceptance of more than $62 billion which would be stretched out over a twenty-year interval following an initial eight-year grace period. To appreciate the scope of the problem, it should be noted that more than three-hundred lending institutions, organized under a steering committee, met for several months with the government's designees in clearing up the repayment problem, sweetened for the creditors by immediate clearance of the nearly $4 billion of arrears to be repaid.

Assorted Other Remnants. For all the furor over the debts issue, human errors and waste or corruption still account for much less in Brazil's case than for that of the other three Latin states with comparable debt burdens—Mexico, Argentina, and Venezuela. According to Geoffrey Smith (1983: 74), from information gathered in interviewing leading industrial, financial, and governmental figures in each state, as much as 80 percent of Brazil's foreign loans have been invested in productive assets, though ultimate value may be long in realization from the $10 billion spent on nuclear power plants, or the $16 billion which were expended in the building of the world's largest hydroelectric dam at Itaipu, on the southern border adjoining Paraguay. Emerging from other "pharaonic" nation-building designs such as those mentioned in chapter 5, Brazil has in reserve industrial modernization and even valuable experience, as part of its difficult emergence into the capitalist Western world of globally oriented major powers.

John Sloan (1984: 212–42), by juxtaposing for purposes of illustration Cuba and Brazil as striking opposites in policy views toward nation-building, found that each had made better use of its opportunities over the past two decades than many Third World neighbors. Even while accumulating enormous debt burdens—for Cuba $526 per capita, and for Brazil $254 per capita—each had done better at creating growth and economic opportunity for its citizens than the others. Sloan concluded (1984: 57) that leaders of other countries had misplaced efforts and caused confusion of direction for their countries by attempting simultaneously to gain economic growth while also increasing income equality through redistribution. To illustrate the futility of that practice, he cited W. Arthur Lewis's analogy of attempting to ride two horses.

Another remnant from authoritarian days has been a new military-industrial complex which the supervisory Armed Forces General Staff (EMFA) Ministry estimated to consist of 350 firms engaged in producing for armed forces purchasers worldwide, and an accompanying military-bureaucracy complex. São Paulo writer João Vitor Strauss, cited in *Latin America Regional Reports, Brazil* (RB 84–10: 5), believes there were as many as forty thousand now retired military men working at second career jobs in government, and an equal or larger number among the over one-hundred thousand workers in the arms production industries. Surrounding the president in advisory capacities and staff support, about one-fourth of the two thousand employed in *Palacio do Planalto* are active members of the armed forces. Another military component, headed by a dozen or more high-ranked officers of the three services and the National Intelligence Service (SNI, which is in effect a fourth paramilitary service), is a sizable staff of "parliamentary liaison" advisers who watch over service interests, including preservation of the protective "market reserve" measures which undergird the neophyte arms industry anticipated to bring in $3 billion in export sales annually (Stepan, 1988: 83).

A final remnant, with ominous potential as a political power center in any future crisis comparable to 1964, as Stepan (1988: 16–23) and Skidmore (1988: 272) have pointed out, is the very large national intelligence network, which at one time permeated every bureaucracy and ministry down to the state level. In that the potential has been known for some time—as its founder, General Golbery said, we created a monster!—recognition and means of superordinated control are forthcoming in the current regime. It is not yet possible to predict an outcome from any future tussle in the arena between a small but determined hard-liner element and freely elected civil authorities. If any insight to the future, is offered by frequent testing of wills and leverage which accompanied the rewriting of the 1988 constitution, I would be inclined to call it a draw. Originally, a determined but unrepresentative drafting committee of the constituent assembly wanted to erase every vestige of legal authority for the military "moderating power" to challenge or overturn constituted authority. It would also have abolished the National Security Council and all elements of the "national security doctrine" which had been instituted in the 1967 constitution and its subsequent amendments. In clear opposition to the expressed will of the military leadership, the Congress also seemed bent upon changing to the parliamentary form of government, enhancing powers for the legislators while trimming back as much as possible the great powers of the executive.

In the end, following heavy posturing and negotiations with what appeared to be a larger *Centrão* (Centrist) coalition in the Congress, the presidential system and quite a bit of the familiar (if unstated) power wielded in past decades by the military elite were written into the new constitution. Moderator authority was grudgingly retained, but only by the concurrence of one of the "three powers" of coequal authority adopted one hundred years ago, in emulation of the U.S. Constitution, i.e., the president, the Congress, and the Supreme Federal Tribunal. The National Security Council was abolished, putting in its stead a National Defense Council with purely advisory authority that would try to bring together the executive and legislative leadership. A final round in the negotiations with the army minister, acting as spokesman for the other military ministers, allowed transfer of the National Security Council's staff secretariat to the National Defense Council, but managed to in effect vacate the role held by the president's right-hand man, the head of Military Staff (*Casa Militar*) who was the secretary general of the former NSC. This to me was the most meaningful decision in redirecting civil-military relationships, since each *Casa Militar* general held enormous power, as the president's closest daily contact with the armed forces.

Conclusions About the "Legacy." The military leadership, in voluntary relinquishment of ruling powers, accepted the fact that it was ill-equipped to continue to direct the affairs of state without great peril to its institutional unity and image. Its fears for the future seem well founded. Past accomplishments which this study has pointed out seem rather hollow, in the face of the stern challenges yet to be faced and conquered, and the impoverishment—however unintended—of the masses of their lower-class countrymen. Even five years afterward, there is insufficient distance from the military era for me to give a fair assessment of the potential of a well-led military regime, using sound and aggressive methods and resources, to take power and lead a country such as Brazil toward its full potential. One may want wistfully to add some apologetics of the "if only . . . " variety, especially concerning economic calamities of the mid-seventies which befell both the First and Third Worlds (save those with petroleum resources). Perhaps, as the adage goes, it was better to have tried and failed than not to have tried at all. Even in failure, there remains room for continued optimism, for which Brazilians are well noted.

List of Acronyms

AÇESITA Itabira Special Steel Company
AÇOMINAS Steel Company of Minas Gerais State
ADESG Alumni Association ESG
AGEBRAS PETROBRAS Management Company
AID (U.S.) Agency for International Development
ALN National Liberator Action
ARENA Alliance for National Renovation (party)

BRASPETRO Petroleum Importation Company of Brazil

CAPEMI Military Personnel Retirement Fund
CCN Commerce and Navigation Company
CDE Economic Development Council
CDI Council of Industrial Development
CEMCFA Major Command and Staff of the Armed Forces Course
CGT General Labor Congress
CHESF Hydroelectric Company of Sõ Francisco Valley
CIDOC Centre for Information and Documentation (Mexico)
CIEX Army Center for Information
CIMETAL International Metallurgic Company
CMN National Monetary Council
CODI-DOI Army Intelligence Center-Division of Special Investigations
COSIPA São Paulo Steel Company
CPRM Mineral Resources Research Company
CSG Curso Superior de Guerra, Senior Course
CSN National Steel Company
CVRD Rio Doçe Valley Company (iron and steel)

DNOCS Drought Works Bureau

ECEME Major Command and Staff School
ELECTROBRAS Brazilian Electric Corporation
EMFA Armed Forces General Staff
ESG Escola Superior de Guerra

FEB Brazilian Expeditionary Force
FSLN *Sandinista* National Liberation Front (Nicaragua)
FUNDECE Fund to Democratize Capital

GATT General Agreement on Trade and Tariffs
GDP gross domestic product
GSP Generalized System of Preferences

IBS Brazilian Iron and Steel Institute
ICOR increments of capital to output ratios
IDB Inter American Development Bank
IMF International Monetary Fund
INTERBRAS Brazilian International Petroleum Company
IPM military police inquiries
ISEB Institute for Socioeconomic Studies of Brazil
ISI import substitution industrialization
ITABIRA Itabira International Company

LIBOR London Interbank Offered Rate

MDB Movement for Brazilian Democracy (party)
MEB Basic Education Movement
MINEROBRAS Brazilian Mineral Extraction Corporation

NATO North Atlantic Treaty Organization

OBAN Operation Bandeirantes

PCB Brazilian Communist Party
PDS Democratic Socialist Party
PETROBRAS Brazilian Petroleum Corporation
PETRODIS PETROBRAS Distribution Company
PETROQUISA PETROBRAS Petroleum Research Company
PIN National Integration Program
PIS Social Integration Program
PLF Liberal Front Party
PMDB Brazilian Democratic Movement Party
PROALCOOL Program for Alcohol Substitution
PTB Brazilian Labor Party

SEPLAN Planning Secretariat
SIDERBRAS Brazilian Steel Institute
SNI National Intelligence Service

STM Supreme Military Court
SUDAM Amazonian Development Superintendency
SUDENE Superintendency for Economic Development of the Northeast

UNE National Students Union
USIBA Steel Refinery Company of Bahia State
USIMINAS Steel Refinery Company of Minas Gerais State

VPR Popular Revolutionary Vanguard

Chronology of Major Events, 1964–1985

April 1–4, 1964: Military leadership declares "revolution" to oust President Goulart. Senate president declares presidency vacant as Goulart flies to his ranch in southernmost state, then to asylum in Uruguay. Constitutional successor as acting president is Chamber President Mazzili. Revolutionary junta formed.

April 11, 1964: Congress ratifies the junta nominee, Castello Branco, as president after junta abrogates constitution, calls election. Purges begin under military boards of inquiry (IPMs).

October 1965: Attempt at semidemocratic rule backfires as two prominent opposition figures are elected to governorships, and a "coup within the Coup" brews, threatening to depose Castello Branco after he insists they will assume elected powers. As a compromise, Castello Branco issues Institutional Act #2, to abolish political parties and direct elections of governors. Other restrictive measures and purgings follow.

February 1966: Institutional Act #3 requires indirect elections of mayors of major cities and state capitals, sets up plans for congressional and state elections for late 1966, and creates the two-party system: ARENA (progovernment) and MDB (loyal opposition). Drafting begins on 1967 Constitution.

November 1966: In second test of public response, ARENA candidates win 70 percent of Chamber and Senate seats. Costa e Silva is elected as next president, campaigning unopposed nationwide.

March 1967: Pledged to "humanize" the revolution, Costa e Silva begins five-year term with a cabinet of military-civilian cast, and a decidedly nationalistic turn away from foreign dominance. Popularity soon ebbs, as strikes, student revolts, rising guerrilla attacks, and a populist civilian "Broad Front" draw attention to the unrest caused by government austerity policies.

December 1968: Costa e Silva issues Institutional Act #5 recessing Congress, after it refuses his demand to authorize punishment of Deputy Moreira Alves for insulting the armed forces. Various IA #5 measures suspend all legal opposition, establish decree rule, and gave the president broad emergency powers.

September 1969: Civilian Vice President Aleixo is prevented from assuming temporary succession when Costa e Silva suffers a severe, disabling stroke (and dies in December). Instead, the military High Command assumes control, dealing with the emergency caused by the kidnapping of U.S. Ambassador Elbrick, amid signs of spreading guerrilla threat to continuation of the authoritarian system. Fifteen captured guerrillas are freed to ransom Elbrick.

October 1969: Presidency is declared vacant, Congress reconvened, and High Command nominee, General Médici, is sworn in for a five-year term. New cabinet members are named and a repressive strategy soon evolves.

November 1970: Congressional elections, which MDB party chooses to boycott (urging blank balloting as a protest), provides ARENA and Médici with overwhelming majority strength, used to promote development and modest popularizing programs, based upon the "miracle years" of economic growth and large revenue surpluses.

March 1974: General Geisel is sworn in as fourth president under suddenly reversing economic fortunes, due to heavy oil dependency.

November 1974: Congressional elections show resurgence of the MDB party.

February–April 1977: Succession conflict begins between Geisel and the hardline faction, with Congress, The Church, and media. (See "Herzog affair" and "Frota affair" in chapter 6.) Geisel closes Congress temporarily to amend constitution by decree, in the "April package," perceived necessary to control the succession.

October 1978: General Figueiredo is elected by a stacked Electoral College (Congress). Geisel undertakes liberalization and ends such authoritarian measures as IA #5 and arbitrary arrests.

March 1979: Figueiredo regime is installed, begins *Abertura* policy with amnesty to political exiles, releases political prisoners, and ends ARENA-MDB two-party restrictions. By March 1980 reorganized Congress has razor-thin progovernment (PDS) majority.

October–November 1981: Figueiredo suffers heart attack, and Aureliano Chaves (civilian vice president), as acting president, guides pro-PDS election rules changes through Congress over a divided opposition.

August–November 1982: Open elections, except for president, bring burst of campaign activism, resulting in no majority in lower chamber of Congress, and prominent antigovernment figures elected to governorships of leading states, notably Brizola (Rio de Janeiro).

January–April 1984: Direct election of president (*Diretas já*) campaign, despite long constitutional odds, sweeps national enthusiasm of opposition to new heights.

July–August 1984: Mixed public-private electioneering for votes in the party conventions and upcoming indirect election end with Maluf winning PDS nomination, but the split of PFL "Liberal Front" bloc to the opposition, and the nomination of moderate Minas Gerais Governor Tancredo Neves to head PMDB-PLF coalition portend Maluf defeat.

January 1985: Neves-Sarney slate of "Democratic Alliance" defeats Maluf-Magalhães Pinto ticket, 480 to 180. Neves begins exhausting overseas trips to resurrect Brazilian economy.

March–April 1985: Neves emergency surgery one day before inauguration, and death April 21 leaves ex-PDS Senate president José Sarney as successor and leader of the redemocratization.

Bibliography

de Andrade, Manuel C. *The Land and the People of the Northeast,* trans. Dennis Johnson. Albuquerque, University of New Mexico Press, 1980.

Arrães, Miguel. *Brazil: The People and the Power*. Trans. Lancelot Sheppard. Harmondsworth, England: Penguin Books, 1972.

de Arruda, Antônio. *A Escola Superior de Guerra*. 20 ed. São Paulo: Edições GRD, Instituto do Livro, 1983.

Associação dos Diplomados da Escola Superior de Guerra (ADESG). *Almanaque*. Rio de Janeiro: ADESG, 1981.

———. *Coleteanos de informações aos participantes dos Ciclos de Estudos*. Rio de Janeiro: ADESG, 1984.

———. *Resumo historico da ADESG*. (Mimeo.) Rio de Janeiro: ADESG, n.d.

Bacchus, Wilfred A. *The Political Dimension of Water Resources Development: A Study of the Brazilian Northeast, 1964–1971*. Ph.D. diss., University of Connecticut, 1973.

———. "Long-term Military Rulership in Brazil: Ideologic Consensus and Dissensus, 1963–1983." *Journal of Political and Military Sociology* 13 (1985): 99–123.

———. "Development Under Military Rule: Factionalism in Brazil." *Armed Forces and Society* 12 (1986): 401–18.

———. "Controlled Political Transition in Brazil: *Abertura* as a Process for a Gradual Sharing of Political Power." In *Liberalization and Redemocratization in Latin America,* ed. George A. Lopez and Michael Stohl. WestPort, Conn.: Greenwood Press, 1987, pp. 137–71.

Bandeira, Moniz. *Presença dos Estados Unidos no Brasil*. Rio de Janeiro: Editôra Civilização Brasileira, 1973.

de Barros, Alexandre S. C. "Back to the Barracks: An Option for the Brazilian Military?" *Third World Quarterly* 7 (1985): 63–77.

Black, Jan K. *United States Penetration of Brazil*. Philadelphia: University of Pennsylvania Press, 1977.

———. "The Military and Political Decompression in Brazil." *Armed Forces and Society* 6 (1980): 625–38.

Burns, E. Bradford. *Nationalism in Brazil*. New York: Praeger, 1968.

Business International. *The New Brazil: Prospects for Stability and Profits*. New York: B.I. Corp., 1965.

———. *Brazil: New Business Power in Latin America*. New York: B.I. Corp., 1971.

Cantril, Hadley. *Patterns of Human Concerns: Brazil*. New Brunswick, N.J.: Rutgers University Press, 1965.

Cardoso, Fernando H. "Associated-Dependent Development: Theoretical and Practical Implications." In *Authoritarian Brazil*, ed. Alfred Stepan. New Haven, Conn.: Yale University Press, 1973, pp. 142–76.

Cardoso, Fernando H., and Enzo Faletto. *Dependency and Development in Latin America*, trans. Marjorie M. Urquidi. Berkley: University of California Press, 1974.

Castello Branco, Humberto de A. "Segurança e Desenvolvimento." Lecture C–01–67, Escola Superior de Guerra, Rio de Janeiro, 13 March 1967.

de Castro, Josüe. *Death in the Northeast*. New York: Vintage, 1969.

Comblin, Joseph. *A ideolôgia de segurança nacional: O poder militar na America Latina*, trans. A. Veiga Filho. 3ª ed. Rio de Janeiro: Editôra Civilização Brasileira, 1980.

do Couto e Silva, Golbery "A estrategia politica." Lecture C–18–54, Escola Superior de Guerra, Rio de Janeiro, 1954.

Costa, Octavio. "Compreensão da Revolução Brasileira." *A Defesa Nacional*. Special Edition September–October 1964: 63–69.

dos Santos, Teotônio. "Brazil: Origins of a Crisis." In *Latin America: The Struggle With Dependency and Beyond*, ed. Ronald Chilcote and Joel Edelstein Cambridge, Mass.: Schenkman, 1974, pp. 415–90.

Dreifuss, Rene. *1964: A conquista do estado*. 3a ed. Petropolis, RJ, Brazil: Editôra Vozes, 1981.

Druckman, Daniel, and Elaine Vaurio. "Regimes and Selection of Political and Military leaders: Brazilian Cabinet Ministers and Generals." *Journal of Political and Military Sociology* 11 #2 (1983): 301–24.

Empresa Brasileira de Noticias. *Autoridades Brasileiras, Edição 84*. Brasilia: EBN, Ministério da Justicia, 1984.

Escola Superior de Guerra. *Manual básico*. Rio de Janeiro: ESG, 1983.

Fagen, Richard R., and Wayne Cornelius, eds. *Political Power in Latin America: Seven Confrontations*. Englewood Cliffs, N.J.: Prentice-Hall, 1978.

Feld, Maury D. "Military Self-Image in a Technological Environment." In *The New Military*, ed. Morris Janowitz. New York: Russell Sage Foundation, 1964, pp. 159–88.

Fiechter, Georges-Andre. *Brazil Since 1964: Modernization Under a Military Regime*. New York: John Wiley, 1975.

Fishlow, Albert. "Some Reflections on Post–1964 Brazilian Economic Policy." In *Authoritarian Brazil*, ed. Alfred Stepan. New Haven, Conn.: Yale University Press, 1973, pp. 69–118.

Flynn, Peter. *Brazil: A Political Study*. Boulder, Col.: Westview, 1979.

Forman, Shepard. *The Brazilian Peasantry*. New York: Columbia Univ. Press, 1975.

Free, Lloyd. *Some International Implications of the Political Psychology of Brazilians*. Princeton, N.J.: Institute for International Social Research, 1961.

Freyre, Gilberto. *Nordeste*. 40 ed. Rio de Janeiro: Editora José Olympio, 1967.

Furtado, Celso. *Brasil: Tempos modernos*. Rio de Janeiro: Editôra Paz e Terra, 1968.

Galeano, Eduardo. "Brazil: The Defeat and After." *Studies on the Left* 4, No. 4 (1964): 55–61.

———. "The De-Nationalization of Brazilian Industry." Monthly Review 21, No. 7 (1969): 11–30.

Gerassi, John. *The Great Fear in Latin America*. Rev. ed. New York: Collier Books, 1965.

Hewitt, Cynthia. "Brazil: The Peasant Movement of Pernambuco, 1961–1964." In *Latin American Peasant Movements*, ed. Henry Landsberger. Ithaca, N.Y.: Cornell Univ. Press, 1969, pp. 374–98.

Hirschman, Albert O. *The Strategy of Economic Development*. New Haven, Conn.: Yale University Press, 1958.

Hoge, Warren. "When Seizing Power Is Easier Than Exercising It." *New York Times*, 23 January 1983, sect. 4, p. E3, col. 8.

Horowitz, Irving L. *Revolution in Brazil: Politics and Society in a Developing Nation*. New York: E. P. Dutton, 1964.

Huntington, Samuel P. *Political Order in Changing Societies*. New Haven, Ct.: Yale University Press, 1968.

———. "Will More Countries Become Democratic?" *Political Science Quarterly* 99 (1984): 193–218.

Instituto Brasileiro de Geografia e Estatistica. *Sinopse estatistica de Brasil, 1972*. English ed. Rio de Janeiro: Servico Grafico, IBGE, 1972.

Interamerican Development Bank. *Economic and Social Progress in Latin America, 1980–81 Report*. Washington: IDB, 1981.

———. *Economic and Social Progress in Latin America, 1985 Report*. Washington, IDB, 1985.

———. *Economic and Social Progress in Latin America, 1986 Report*. Washington: IDB, 1986.

Jaguaribe, Hêlio. "Brasil:" Estabilidade social pelo colonial-fascismo? In *Brasil: Tempos modêrnos*, ed. Celso Furtado Rio de Janeiro: Editôra Paz e Terra, 1968, pp. 25–47.

Janowitz, Morris. *The Professional Soldier* Glencoe, Ill.: Free Press, 1960.

———. *The Military in the Political Development of the New Nations*. Chicago: University of Chicago Press, 1964.

Johnson, Allen W. *Sharecroppers of the Sertão*. Stanford, Calif.: Stanford University Press, 1971.

Julião, Francisco. *Brasil, antes y despues*. Mexico City: Editorial Nuestro Tiempo, 1968.

———. *Cambão-The Yoke: The Hidden Face of Brazil*, Trans. John Butt. Harmondsworth, England: Penguin Books, 1972.

Jurema, Abelardo. *Seixta-feira, 13: As ultimas dias do governo João Goulart*. 3ª ed. Rio de Janeiro: Edições Cruzeiro, 1964.

de Kadt, Emanuel. *Catholic Radicals in Brazil*. London: Oxford University Press, 1970.

Krieger, Robert A. *Brazil: A Special Economic Study*. New York: First National City Bank, 1971.

Lambert, Jacques. *Os dois Brasis*. Rio de Janeiro: Editôra Civilização Brasileira, 1959.

Latin America (London). "Gathering Clouds for a Rain." IX, No. 38 (1975): 302.

———. "Troubled Times." IX, No. 44 (1975): 346–48.

———. "Geisel Recovers." X, No. 2 (1976): 14–15.

Latin America Political Report (London). "General Frota: The Loser in the Palace Coup." XI, No. 41 (1977): 323.

Latin America Regional Reports, Brazil (London). "New Questions on Income Distribution." RB 80–04 (1980): 6–7.

———. "More Accusations From the Grave." RB 83–04 (1983): 3.

———. "Soldiers Legacy to the Civilians." RB 84–10 (1984): 5.

———. "Figueiredo Returns to Political Arena." RB 87–08 (1987): 3.

———. "Debate on Army's 'Internal' Role." RB 88–09 (1988): 7.

Latin America Weekly Report (London). "Neves Meets Armed Forces Ministers." WR 84–48 (1984): 8.

Lernoux, Peggy. *Cry of the People*. Harmondsworth, England: Penguin Books, 1982.

Lipset, Seymour M. "Some Social Requisites of Democracy: Economic Development and Political Legitimacy." *American Political Science Review* 53 (1959): 69–105.

———. *Political Man: The Social Bases of Politics*, 2nd. ed. Baltimore: Johns Hopkins University Press, 1981.

Loveman, Brian, and Thomas E. Davies, eds. *The Politics of Antipolitics*. Lincoln: University of Nebraska Press, 1978.

Lowenthal, Abraham F. *Brazil and the United States*. New York: Foreign Policy Assn., 1986.

Macridis, Roy. *Modern Political Regimes: Patterns and Institutions*. Boston: Little, Brown, 1986.

Manwaring, Max G. "Career Patterns and Attitudes of MilitaryPolitical Elites in Brazil: Similarities and Continuity, 1964–1975." *International Journal of Contemporary Sociology* 19 (1978): 235–50.

Markoff, John, and Silvio R. Duncan Baretta. "Professional Ideology and Military Activism in Brazil." *Comparative Politics* 17 (1985): 175–91.

McCann, Frank D. "Origins of the New Professionalism" of the Brazilian Military. *Journal of InterAmerican Studies and World Affairs* 21 (1979): 505–22.

McDonough, Peter. *Power and Ideology in Brazil*. Princeton, N.J.: Princeton University Press, 1981.

Mendes de A., Candido. "Elites de poder, democrácia e desenvolvimento." *Dados* 6 (1969): 57–90.

———. *Beyond Populism*, trans. L. Gray Cowan. Albany, N.Y.: SUNY Press, 1977.

Mikes, George. *Tango: A Solo Across South America*. London: Andre Deutsch, 1961.

Morel, Edmar. *O golpe començou en Washington*. Rio de Janeiro: Editôra Civilização Brasileira, 1965.

Moss, Robert. *The Moving Frontier: A Survey of Brazil*. London: *The Economist*, Survey Report, 1972.

Nordlinger, Eric. *Soldiers and Politics*. Englewood Cliffs, N.J.: Prentice-Hall, 1977.

O'Donnell, Guillermo. *Modernization and Bureaucratic-Authoritarianism: Studies in South American Politics*. Berkeley: Univ. of California Press, 1973.

O'Donnell, Guillermo, Philippe C. Schmitter, and Laurence Whitehead, eds. *Transitions From Authoritarian Rule: Prospects for Democracy, Vol. IV*. Baltimore: Johns Hopkins University Press, 1986.

Page, Joseph A. *The Revolution That Never Was: Northeast Brazil, 1955–1964*. New York: Grossman, 1972.

Palmeira, Moacir. "The Aftermath of Peasant Mobilization: Rural Conflicts in the Brazilian Northeast Since 1964." In *The Structure of Brazilian Development*, ed. Neuma Aguiar. New Brunswick, N.J.: Transaction Press, 1979, pp. 71–97.

Pang, Eul-soo, and Laura Jarnagin. "A Requiem for Authoritarianism in Brazil." *Current History* 84, No. 494 (1985): 61–64, 88–89.

Parker, Phyllis. *O papel dos Estados Unidos no golpe de estado de 31 de Março*. Rio de Janeiro: Editôra Civilização Brasileiro, 1977.

"Pau de Arara" (Pseudonym). *La violencia militar en el Brasil*. Mexico City: Editora Siglo XXI, 1972.

Pearson, Neale. *Small Farmer and Rural Pressure Groups in Brazil* Ph.D. dissertation, University of Florida, 1967.

Pedreira, Fernando. *Março 31: Civis e militares no processo da crise Brasileira*. Rio de Janeiro: Editôra José Alvaro, 1964.

Pereira, Osny Duarte. *A Transamazônica: Prós e contras*. 2a ed. Rio de Janeiro: Editôra Civilização Brasileira, 1971.

Quartim, Joao. *Dictatorship and Armed Struggle in Brazil*, trans. David Fernbach. New York: Monthly Review Press, 1971.

Republica do Brasil. *Mêtas e bases para a ação do govêrno*. Rio de Janeiro: Serviço Grafico, IBGE, 1970.

Ribeiro, Belisa. *Bomba no Riocentro*. 2a ed. Rio de Janeiro: Editôra Codecri, 1982.

Riding, Alan. "A Democracy That Suits the Generals." *New York Times*, April 10, 1988, p. E–1.

———. "For Brazil's Political Elite, Rock-Bottom Ratings." *New York Times*, March 7, 1989, p. 12.

Roett, Riordan. *Brazil: Politics in a Patrimonial Society*. New York: Praeger Publishers, 1972.

Rostow, Walt W. *The Stages of Economic Growth*. Cambridge, England: Cambridge University Press, 1964.

Sales Grande, Eurico A. "O exército e o ensino superior." *A Defesa Nacional*, No. 705 (1983): 141–61.

Schmitter, Philippe C. "The 'Portugalization' of Brazil?" In *Authoritarian Brazil*, ed. Alfred Stepan. New Haven, Conn.: Yale University Press, 1973, pp. 179–232.

Schneider, Ronald M. *The Political System of Brazil*. New York: Columbia Univ. Press, 1971.

———. *Brazil: Foreign Policy of a Future World Power*. Boulder, Colo.: Westview Press, 1976.

SEPLAN, Republica do Brasil. *Consolidação plurianual de programas do govêrno, 1982–85*. Brasilia: Secretaria de Planejamento, 1982.

Siegel, Gilbert B. "Brazil: Diffusion and Centralization of Power." In *Development Administration in Latin America*, ed. Clarence Thurber and Lawrence S. Graham. Durham, N.C.: Duke University Press, 1973, pp. 362–81.

Skidmore, Thomas E. *Politics in Brazil, 1930–1964*. New York: Oxford University Press, 1967.

———. "Politics and Economic Policy Making in Authoritarian Brazil, 1937–71." In *Authoritarian Brazil*, ed. Alfred Stepan. New Haven, Conn.: Yale University Press, 1973, pp. 3–46.

———. *The Politics of Military Rule in Brazil, 1964–85*. New York: Oxford University Press, 1988.

Sloan, John W. *Public Policy in Latin America*. Pittsburg: University of Pittsburgh Press, 1984.

Smith, Geoffrey. "South American Debt–Now Look at the Assets." *Forbes* 131, No. 12 (June 6, 1983): 73–78.

Sola Pool, Ithiel de. *Trends in Content Analysis*. Urbana: University of Illinois Press, 1959.

Stepan, Alfred. *The Military in Politics: Changing Patterns in Brazil*. Princeton, N.J.: Princeton University Press, 1971.

———. "The New Professionalism of Internal Warfare and Military Role Expansion." In *Authoritarian Brazil*, ed. Alfred Stepan. New Haven, Conn.: Yale University Press, 1973, pp. 47–65.

———. "Political Leadership and Regime Breakdown: Brazil." In *Latin America: The Breakdown of Democratic Regimes*, eds. Juan J. Linz and Alfred Stepan. Baltimore: Johns Hopkins University Press, 1978a, pp. 110–37.

———. *The State and Society: Peru in Comparative Perspective*. Princeton, N.J.: Princeton University Press, 1978b.

———. *Rethinking Military Politics: Brazil and the Southern Cone*. Princeton, N.J.: Princeton University Press, 1988.

Távora, Juarez do N. "A segurança naçional, a política, e a estratégia." Lecture A–01–53, Escola Superior de Guerra, Rio de Janeiro, 14 March 1953.

Taylor, Kit S. *Sugar and Underdevelopment of Northeast Brazil, 1500–1970*. (Mimeo.) Gainesville: University of Florida Press, 1978.

Tullis, F. LeMond. *Modernization in Brazil*. Provo, Utah: Brigham Young University Press, 1973.

Uys, Errol L. *Brazil*. New York: Simon and Schuster, 1986.

Wagley, Charles W. *An Introduction to Brazil*. New York: Columbia University Press, 1963.

Wesson, Robert, ed. *U.S. Influence in Latin America in the 1980s*. New York: Praeger Publishers, 1982.

Willkie, Mary E. *Rural Syndicates in Pernambuco*. Rio de Janeiro: Conselho Latinoamericano de Pesquisas e Estudos Sociais, 1964.

World Bank. *World Development Report, 1984*. Washington: IBRD, 1984a.

———. *Brazil: A Country Study*. Washington: IBRD, 1984b.

Wyckoff, Theodore. "The Role in the Military in Latin American Politics." In

The Dynamics of Change in Latin American Politics, ed. John D. Martz. Englewood Cliffs, N.J.: Prentice-Hall, 1965, pp. 263–75.

Young, Jordan M. *Brazil, 1954–64: End of a Civilian Cycle*. New York: Facts on File, 1972.

Index

About the Author

WILFRED A. BACCHUS is a Professor in the Department of Political Science at Muhlenberg College. Previously he served on the faculties of the University of Connecticut, Southern Connecticut State University, Sacred Heart University, and the Naval War College.